Battle for the Firstborn

Cover Design by Mary Nell Lee
Background artwork- François-Charles Cécile/ Public Domain
Photograph of Tutankhamun's Middle Coffin- A. Parrot/ CC BY-SA

Battle
for the
Firstborn
*The Exodus and the
Death of Tutankhamun*

Mary Nell Wyatt

Foreword by Scott Parvi

Royal Hill Press

Royal Hill Press
3413 Greens Mill Rd.
Spring Hill, TN. 37174

Contents

PREFACE

I wrote this book to fulfill a promise I made to my late husband, Ron Wyatt, who passed away in 1999. Ron devoted his life to work he believed God chose him to do- to search for and reveal evidence God had preserved which confirm the absolute validity and accuracy of the Biblical account.

Ron Wyatt 1933-1999

During his lifetime, he was not taken seriously because he was not an educated scholar but he never let that deter nor discourage him. In fact, almost all professional scholars, archaeologists and scientists would not even examine his evidences. They instead wrote articles criticizing him and ridiculing his discoveries.

Before he died in August of 1999, Ron said to me, "When I am gone, they will have to deal with the evidence." That statement has come to fruition. Today, his discoveries in Turkey, Egypt and Saudi Arabia are now accepted by many as Noah's Ark, the true Red Sea crossing site and the real Mount Sinai.

It has been the greatest honor of my life to be allowed to be involved in this work with Ron. The subject of this book was the first project that Ron gave me. He told me his beliefs concerning the chronology of the 18th Dynasty as the time of the Exodus and he asked me to research and show how it fit together in a cohesive model. I worked for a stock broker where I was the senior options principal when we met and as a mathematically inclined person, I was a methodical researcher and looked forward to the task. I accepted the assignment with excitement and enthusiasm even though the subject was completely new to me at the time.

Beginning with the knowledge that all dates in ancient Egypt were given in the year of a pharaoh's reign, I began to try to piece events together. It was a long journey for me. I knew it would be difficult to present the data in a manner than was understandable to the average person who had no background in ancient Egyptian history like myself when I began this project. I also believe that God had a time for this to be presented and I was deeply impressed a few months ago that it was time.

It was always Ron's desire to make all of his work available to anyone who was interested. Due to the complexity of this subject, a book was the only way it could be presented.

To view video of Ron's research and discoveries, you can go to our YouTube Channel, ronwyatt.com, at https://www.youtube.com/c/ronwyattcom.

The Ron Wyatt family website can be seen at www.ronwyatt.com.

FOREWARD

by Scott Parvi

For many decades people around the world have been intrigued by the history of Egypt. From the majestic pyramids of Giza, one of the "Seven Wonders of the World," to the amazing discovery and treasures of King Tut's tomb, the world has stood in awe of what must have transpired in ancient times along the banks of the Nile River. Many books have been written and many movies have been made to try and bring clarity to the life and times of this fascinating part of the world which predates most other civilizations.

One book that is often overlooked by Egyptologists, scholars and scientists, which contains a plethora of knowledge of those times, is the Bible. The Bible is often discounted as a collection of myths and fables which does nothing more than tantalize our curiosity of the past rather than provide an accurate record of historical events.

In the 1956 epic film titled, "The Ten Commandments," produced, directed and narrated by Cecil B. DeMille, the world got its first Technicolor view of what Egypt might have been like according to the Biblical record. Although the film did a somewhat respectable job of portraying the story of the Israelites' exodus from Egypt, it did little to connect the Bible with the archaeological record found during our modern era. In fact, even though it propelled the acting careers of Charlton Heston who played Moses and Yul Brynner who portrayed the pharaoh Rameses I, it did not accurately align who those ancient characters actually were in the forensic records of Egypt. If anything, it caused all the attention to focus on Egypt's 19th Dynasty as the time of the exodus when Rameses I ruled rather than where the actual evidence points to which is the 18th Dynasty. This book does an amazing job of connecting all the dots in the Bible to those found in the sand covered tombs of Egyptian history.

The author of this book, Mary Nell Wyatt Lee writing as Mary Nell Wyatt, takes the reader on an amazing journey through the annals of time to discover how miraculously the Biblical record aligns with the evidence found in the pharaonic record. She credits her late husband, Ron Wyatt, for doing all the research on this topic years earlier and had tasked her with documenting the information which resulted in this book. Of course, it was Ron who always gave credit to God, for the revelations he had been given, to be able to do the pointing in the first place.

Today we are taught that evolution is fact and what the mainstream scientists say is the gospel truth. But that is a mere smokescreen for what truly has taken place in world history often times. This book takes one element of that history found in the massive amount of Egyptian antiquities of the dead and brings to life the Biblical story of the exodus. You will discover many things in this book such as what events in history led up to the time of Israel's captivity in Egypt, who was the pharaoh during the time Moses was rescued from the Nile River, who was the pharaoh's daughter that saved and adopted Moses, who was Moses in actual recorded Egyptian history, who was the ruling pharaoh when Moses led the people of Israel out of Egypt, why King Tutankhamun (Tut) was never really ever a king after all and died in the Passover plague of the firstborn, and the finding of the "real" Mount Sinai in northwest Saudi Arabia in the land of Midian. These, along with many other details, are closely examined with the records found in the ancient tombs, stelae and monuments found in Egypt and elsewhere around the world.

The amount of research that went into the writing of this book is exhausting but the reward for what it uncovered flies in the face of those who would be critics of the Bible and its stories. From when one of Israel's (Jacob's) twelve sons, Joseph, was taken to Egypt as a slave, through when Israel entered the promised land at Jericho, the author makes known to the reader the historical evidence which supports each and every Biblical story in between.

There can be no doubt we have been erroneously taught to ignore these stories as fact by the secular media and institutions. Also, as is often said, "they can't see the forest for the trees," likewise most archaeologists haven't been able to properly identify "the pharaohs for the leaves" of recorded books on Egyptian history.

I think this book clears the air on who each and every pharaoh of the 18th Dynasty was and the role they played in the story of the exodus. There can be no doubt that skeptics will continue to scoff but the truth is not only found in the Bible but also in the stone and stelae which can no longer be ignored. Literally, the rocks are crying out in these Last Days!

After many years of careful study of the evidence available today in Egypt and elsewhere, Mary Nell has compiled it in a manner similar to a jigsaw puzzle by first identifying the edge pieces then filling in the rest with the facts found as well as with the Biblical narrative. If some people have doubted the Bible and if the Israelites ever dwelt in the land of the pharaohs based upon the accepted norms of most so called "scholars" today, they will undoubtedly discover their new found faith in the Word of God as an infallible record of days gone by. Even if you have a mere casual interest in archaeology or Egyptology you will be enthralled with the information brought forth in this masterpiece of methodical evidence nobody has been able to assemble until now.

Finally, a quote taken from the fore mentioned movie, "The Ten Commandments," as the pharaoh often said, "so let it be written, so let it be done," can be taken in light of the Bible. The Bible affords us the ability to not only understand what has transpired in the past but to also know what will occur in the future. If God has written it, it either has or surely will be done!

As you read this book, enjoy the fascinating journey as the mystery of the ancient Egyptians and the story of the Exodus are exposed in the light of the truth.

INTRODUCTION

Deu 29:29 The secret things belong unto the LORD our God: but those things which are revealed belong unto us and to our children for ever, that we may do all the words of this law.

The subject of this book is the Exodus from Egypt and the evidences which validate the Biblical account. It was a monumental battle for Ron the entire time he was involved with his research and field work. But it is my profound belief that God opened many things to his understanding and used him to reveal wonderful evidences of the Truth of His Holy Word.

In the course of my many years of study on this subject, I have learned almost all leading archaeologists and scholars scoff at the Bible as having any historical relevance. As a result, the mainstream archaeological and scholarly world proclaim loudly there is no evidence of the Biblical Exodus.

I believe God gave Ron an understanding concerning ancient Egyptian history that has provided a perfect picture of the Exodus. In addition to the evidence which documents the Egyptian identities involved with Moses and the Exodus, I have chosen to present the events of Ron's discovery of Mount Sinai in Saudi Arabia as evidence of the unseen battle between the Truth of God's Word and the darkness that seeks to blind the world. The only thing that kept Ron encouraged to continue was seeing how the revelations God was making through his work were bringing souls to Him.

Numerous books have been written about the discoveries of Ron Wyatt. The most significant book is "The Exodus Case" by Dr. Lennart Moller with the Karolinska Institute in Sweden. Ron and Lennart were to co-write a book on Ron's research and discoveries but Ron died before it could be written. Lennart then came to me and asked to continue to write the book, explaining that he had the credentials to get Ron's work accepted by the scholarly world. I wanted Ron's life work known to the world so I signed a contract with Lennart, turning over all of Ron's basic research and data.

Lennart published a well-written book entitled "The Exodus Case" with only one brief mention of Ron and it became a popular standard for Christians interested in the Exodus and early Biblical history. The result was that the readers associated Lennart with the work, not the man who made the discoveries. The truth of how these discoveries came to light needs to be known so people realize this was done by the Great I Am and not by any man.

Ron knew it was not his intelligence or wisdom that resulted in the discoveries he made and he never accepted any credit. He felt blessed and honored to be, as he called it, "hands and feet" for whatever God had for him to do. No glory is to be given to anyone except our Creator, the God of Abraham.

But most importantly, the Biblical significance of the discoveries must be given with the evidence. It was Ron's belief that God preserved these things for this point in earth's history as a last pleading to mankind to come to Him and be saved. I believe most Christians today realize that the time is near for the end of all things.

My hope is that the information in this book will strengthen the faith of believers because we will need an unshakable faith to weather the terrible times that lie ahead. I also pray that those who have rejected the Bible as having any validity will see the truth- that the Bible is completely true from beginning to end and decide to take their stand with the believers.

Chapter 1

IMPORTANCE of the EXODUS

Did the Exodus really happen? If so, did it happen like the Bible says or was it something more mundane, like a migration of people over time that grew into a more exciting story as related in the Biblical account? Even among Biblical scholars, there is great debate over this very subject.

Who was Moses and who was pharaoh's daughter who rescued him from the Nile River? Surely with all the ancient remains and artifacts in Egypt, there is something to provide at least some little tidbit of evidence- isn't there? To read the ancient history books, there isn't.

Is it acceptable for a Christian to want to see some evidence? What about faith? Isn't that all I need? Does it offend God if I want some proof?

From the beginning of the evolutionary theory, modern day man has discarded the Biblical story of life and our Creator and opted for the idea that the earth sprang up from chaos over millions of years. All the sacrifices of the early Christians to guard the Word of God with their lives were thrown aside. The Bible was relegated to the historical fiction aisle of the library by most scholars and scientists.

In the time since this theory became generally accepted, leading scholars and scientists developed their own timelines and methods of dating world history which extend far before the Biblical timeline. This has caused confusion for the believer in the Bible and has caused many to actually lose their faith in the Word of God.

The historical evidences from ancient Egypt are many but still lacking in the things which provide a complete account of what actually occurred. Evidence must be interpreted within a context that is valid. This is very difficult for ancient events where there isn't a calendar which relates to time as we know it. It must also coincide with the history of the other nations involved with them at that time.

Ron Wyatt was convinced the Exodus took place during the 18th dynasty of ancient Egypt. He arrived at a major conclusion that changed everything- he concluded that most pharaohs of that dynasty had two different names instead of the commonly accepted theory that each name represented a completely different pharaoh. His premise was that a pharaoh would come to the throne as a co-regent and be given one name. Then when he became the senior pharaoh he was given another name.

In 1988 when I married Ron, he gave me my first assignment, to thoroughly research the 18th dynasty and document how the data fits together within his theory. I began with a chart of the chronology of the 18th Dynasty. With this tool, I spent many years matching dated events with different pharaohs.

As the information came together, I was overwhelmed at how perfectly the data fit the account of the Exodus given in the Bible. I was also frustrated when I learned how antagonistic the scholarly world was towards the Bible. Evidence which clearly proved a Biblical connection almost seemed to be misinterpreted to purposefully deny any relevance.

I have tremendous respect and gratitude for the work of archaeologists, linguists, and all others in the past who made the discoveries of ancient Egypt and translated the monuments and inscriptions. I'm in awe of their knowledge but I respectfully suggest that their interpretation based on what has been found is flawed because their current accepted theory has not been based on the Biblical account.

When the abundance of evidence is scrutinized within the context of the Biblical record, the story comes to life. This book will take the reader through the historical events which led up to the Exodus. You will learn the commonly held beliefs about the Hyksos invading Egypt actually do not align with the evidence. In addition, the strong evidence for which pharaoh's daughter rescued Moses from the Nile River and who she was in the Egyptian records will be laid out. You will also be introduced to the amazing individual in ancient Egyptian history who perfectly fits the life and profile of Moses.

Not only that, but you will be presented the evidence which indicates the famous King Tut never ruled as an emperor pharaoh but died at the hand of the angel who took the lives of the firstborn just before the children of Israel were allowed to leave Egypt. The fascinating story of Tutankhamun's tomb reveals clues which point directly to the cataclysmic events Egypt experienced as a result of the events of the Exodus. Finally, you will come to know who his father was in the list of pharaohs who ruled Egypt and how he met his fate in the Red Sea.

Events Leading to the Exodus

The story of the Exodus is important to every Christian. To say, "I am a New Testament Christian" and disregard the Old Testament, deprives a Christian of the rich heritage which is a vital part of the story of our salvation.

There is much to glean from even the slightest of details throughout the Scriptures. The story of the Exodus, if just an object lesson, is very interesting but what is the real point? If the story is true, down to the most minute of details, it is one of the most amazing events in all of human history.

To fully comprehend the Exodus, we must go back to Genesis. The knowledge of the coming Saviour was known from the time Adam sinned. At that time, God instituted the blood sacrifices which pointed to Jesus' death.

Abraham understood what must occur, as Jesus said to the Jews:

Joh. 8:56 Your father Abraham rejoiced to see my day: and he saw it, and was glad.

The descendants of Abraham through Isaac were to be God's people and one day become the children of Israel. They were chosen because of Abraham's faith and the promise made to him.

The events of the Exodus were part of the unfolding plan of salvation for downfallen man that was decided before the foundation of the earth. God was intervening to prepare the people He chose to preserve the true knowledge of Him and take that knowledge to the world.

Our Creator did nothing without purpose. Every detail of every event is rich with meaning. To fully comprehend the Exodus, it is necessary to understand "the rest of the story," as Paul Harvey used to say.

The Sacrificial System

By the time of the Exodus, the children of Israel had lived in Egypt a long time and were exposed to idolatry and the superstitions of the Egyptians in spite of the fact they remained a separate people. The Egyptians offered sacrifices to their multitude of gods to appease them.

To counter these pagan beliefs, God would give the children of Israel precise instructions concerning His sacrificial system to ensure they understood its meaning. Every act in this system consisted of types which pointed to the True Sacrifice which would take away the sins of the world.

God wanted to keep constantly before them the fact that the consequence of sin required blood.

Lev. 17:11 For the life of the flesh is in the blood: and I have given it to you upon the altar to make an atonement for your souls: for it is the blood that maketh an atonement for the soul.

The Ten Commandments

After the Israelites left bondage in Egypt and came to the mountain God had chosen, Mount Sinai, a covenant was made between God and the great multitude. God gave His unchangeable perfect Law, the Ten Commandments. To show they were immutable and would never be done away with, He wrote them with His own finger in stone and spoke them Himself in the hearing of all the people at Mount Sinai. The multitude signified their acceptance when they all answered in one voice, *"All the words which the Lord hath said we will do."* This covenant was ratified when sacrifices were made on the altar at the foot of Mount Sinai. They were now officially God's chosen people.

God at this time gave precise directions for His sacrificial system, also called the ceremonial law. Each day the people of Israel would bring their sacrifice and while placing their hand upon the innocent little animal, they confessed their sin. This symbolically transferred the sin to the victim which was slain. The priest sprinkled the blood before the veil, behind which was the Ark of the Covenant with the Law of God. This transferred symbolically the sin to the sanctuary where all the confessed sins accumulated.

The Day of Atonement

The Day of Atonement occurred once a year. Two goats were selected for this ceremony: one was "for the Lord" and the other was the "scapegoat." The goat "for the Lord" was slain and its blood was brought into the Most Holy Place and sprinkled on the Mercy Seat of the Ark of the Covenant, which sat above the two Tables of Stone with God's immutable Law.

The blood was also sprinkled on the altar of incense which represents the prayers of the people. The Day of Atonement was the only time the Ark of the Covenant was used. On that day the high priest would put his hands on the live scapegoat and confess all the sins of the people. By this

William James Webb/ Public Domain.

action, the confessed sins of the people were symbolically removed from the sanctuary and placed on the head of the live scapegoat which was led into the wilderness, nevermore to return. In this yearly service the work of Jesus was represented, as both our High Priest and as our sacrifice.

This ceremonial law would one day meet its antitype when Jesus was crucified. His death and shed Blood fulfilled the penalty for all confessed sins as portrayed in the sanctuary service. When type met antitype, all sacrifices were to cease. This is the law Jesus "took ... out of the way, nailing it to the cross." (Col. 2:14) Jesus was the only sacrifice that could pay for the sins of sinful man because He was without sin and His life was His to give.

The Purpose of the Children of Israel

This nation called Israel was to be the "light" to all nations. Through them was the knowledge of the One True God to radiate throughout the world. The invitation to "come to Him" was open to all mankind. God had allowed the children of Israel to experience being in bondage to the Egyptians so they would have a tender heart towards the "stranger" who was not one of them:

Lev. 19:34 But the stranger that dwelleth with you shall be unto you as one born among you, and thou shalt love him as thyself; for ye were strangers in the land of Egypt: I am the LORD your God.

Over 1,400 years later, the Messiah, who was foreshadowed in the ceremonial system, came to the "House of Israel" as prophesied. His earthly ministry was directed to the Jewish nation only. When He called His twelve disciples, He told them:

MAT. 10:6 ... Go not into the way of the Gentiles,... But go rather to the lost sheep of the house of Israel.

He was preparing the children of Israel to take the Gospel to the world, the work they had been chosen to do from the time of Abraham. The faithful followers of Christ took the Gospel message of salvation through the shed Blood of Jesus to the Jewish nation first. After about three and a half years, though many accepted salvation through Christ, the nation of Israel as a whole rejected it.

Acts 13:46 Then Paul and Barnabas waxed bold, and said, It was necessary that the word of God should first have been spoken to you: but seeing ye put it from you, and judge yourselves unworthy of everlasting life, lo, we turn to the Gentiles.

The faithful followers of Jesus then took the Gospel to the Gentile world. And no greater feat has ever occurred on earth. To understand more correctly what had occurred, in Romans chapter 11, we read the parable of how the "branches," or natural Jews, were broken off the olive tree because of their unbelief while the Gentile "branches" who believed in the Messiah were grafted in. As salvation had been available to the "stranger" during the days of the Old Testament, so too was salvation still available to the Jew as well as the Gentile. And so it remains until today. It all goes back to Abraham whose faithfulness caused God to bless him and the entire world through his "seed":

GAL. 27 For as many of you as have been baptized into Christ have put on Christ. 28 There is neither Jew nor Greek, there is neither bond nor free, there is neither male nor female: for ye are all one in Christ Jesus. 29 And if ye be Christ's, then are ye Abraham's seed, and heirs according to the promise.

The Old Testament is our heritage just as is the New Testament. The Messiah of Christians today is the same Saviour Who spoke to ancient Israel:

Isa. 48:16 ...I have not spoken in secret from the beginning; from the time that it was, there am I: and now the Lord GOD, and his Spirit, hath sent me. 17 Thus saith the LORD, thy Redeemer, the Holy One of Israel; I am the LORD thy God which teacheth thee to profit, which leadeth thee by the way that thou shouldest go.

To stress the importance of our knowledge and understanding of the events of the Exodus, Paul stated:

1Co. 10:11...they are written for our admonition, upon whom the ends of the world are come.

We, as believers, must have complete confidence in the Word of God precisely as He preserved the Scriptures for us. Ron believed God has revealed evidences which prove the total reliability of His Holy Word. These evidences are intended to strengthen the faith of the believer and also draw the non-believer to investigate the Word of God. The hope is when they can see evidence of His Truth, they will join the ranks of the honest-hearted believers of the True God.

As the evidence of the Exodus began to unfold before me while I was researching for Ron, I realized how amazing our God is. He arranged for the evidence to be so clear yet so mystifying at the same time.

The key to understanding all along was the Bible. Without it, we have no basis upon which to build, no starting point.

Chapter 2

Date and Dynasty
of the Exodus

This chapter will cover the evidences which led Ron to his conclusion that the 18th dynasty of Egypt was when the Exodus occurred. The main evidence was his finding chariot parts in the Gulf of Aqaba which dated to that dynasty. Another discovery was evidence of the true Mount Sinai in Saudi Arabia discussed in chapter 18.

The resulting timeline based on his proposed interpretation provides a complete chronology of events prior to Moses' birth down to the death of pharaoh's firstborn. His conclusions were a departure from the accepted ideas and provide the entire picture.

A number of writers have recognized the 18th Dynasty as the most likely one in which the Exodus took place. However, the number of years of reign for each pharaoh made it impossible to arrange the events in a manner which fulfilled the Biblical account. Ron's proposal resolved this issue which will be shown later.

The examination of evidence has to begin with the events that led up to the Exodus as well as the evidences which convinced Ron of the 18th dynasty. Everything in the Bible, both Old and New Testaments, are one continuous chain of events. The Exodus didn't come up as an afterthought, it was part of the unending chain that began with creation.

1Ki. 6:1 And it came to pass in the four hundred and eightieth year after the children of Israel were come out of the land of Egypt, in the fourth year of Solomon's reign over Israel, in the month Zif, which is the second month, that he began to build the house of the LORD.

It is an established and generally accepted fact that the date of the 4th year of Solomon's reign would be 967/966 BC. 480 years earlier would place the date of the Exodus at 1447/1446 BC.

430 Years of Exodus 12:40

Another Scriptural event date has to be established to also fit into the date of the Exodus, the four hundred and thirty years of sojourning of the children of Israel:

Exo .12:40 Now the sojourning of the children of Israel, who dwelt in Egypt, was four hundred and thirty years. 41 And it came to pass at the end of the four hundred and thirty years, even the selfsame day it came to pass, that all the hosts of the LORD went out from the land of Egypt.

Paul in Galatians gives a statement which makes clear the event which marked the beginning of the 430 years:

*Gal. 3:16 Now to Abraham and his seed were the promises made. He saith not, And to seeds, as of many; but as of one, And to thy seed, which is Christ. 17 And this I say, [that] **the covenant, that was confirmed before of God in Christ, the law, which was four hundred and thirty years after,** cannot disannul, that it should make the promise of none effect.*

This tells us that the event 430 years before the giving of the law concerned Abraham. God called Abraham to go to a mountain in Moriah and sacrifice his son, Isaac, on an altar they would build together. Because Abraham was obedient to God right up until the Angel of the Lord stopped him from killing his son at the very last second, a promise was made to Abraham:

Gen. 22:15 And the angel of the LORD called unto Abraham out of heaven the second time, 16 And said, By myself have I sworn, saith the LORD, for because thou hast done this thing, and hast not withheld thy son, thine only [son] 17 That in blessing I will bless thee, and in multiplying I will multiply thy seed as the stars of the heaven, and as the sand which [is] upon the sea shore; and thy seed shall possess the gate of his enemies; 18 And in thy seed shall all the nations of the earth be blessed; because thou hast obeyed my voice.

The time of Abraham's seed or offspring, beginning with his son Isaac, until the Exodus would be 430 years, after which the law would be given. It may seem an unimportant issue to some, but every statement given in the Bible is there for a Divine purpose.

Philippe de Champaigne/ Public Domain

Sometimes, a story in the Bible just seems like an old story we have heard so many times in our life. Then one day, something will suddenly be opened to you in a new light. That has been the case with me as I wrote this book and looked at the dates of events for this chapter. In studying about the call of Abraham to take his son, Isaac, and go to a place God would determine and sacrifice his son, a very special insight was revealed.

Importance of Isaac

There is a very important point to be understood concerning Isaac's age when this 430 years began. Since Isaac's death was in 1716 BC, he would have been 20 years old when Abraham was called by God to offer him.

The significance of Isaac's age has great meaning. To understand why this is important to our understanding, we must let the Bible explain. In Numbers 1:3 God told Moses to number or count the men from age 20 years and older to go to war. This was the age they were considered old enough to be soldiers:

Exo. 30:11 And the LORD spake unto Moses, saying, 12 When thou takest the sum of the children of Israel after their number, **then shall they give every man a ransom for his soul unto the LORD,** *when thou numberest them; that there be no plague among them, when [thou] numberest them. 13 This they shall give, every one that passeth among them that are numbered, half a shekel after the shekel of the sanctuary: (a shekel [is] twenty gerahs:) an half shekel [shall be] the offering of the LORD. 14 Every one that passeth among them that are numbered, from twenty years old and above, shall give an offering unto the LORD.*

Those who "shall give, ... a ransom for his soul unto the Lord," implies accountability on the part of the individuals in the above passage who were 20 years old and older. Another strong evidence is seen in the fact those 20 years and older who murmured against the Lord were denied entry into the promised land after the Exodus:

Num. 14:29 Your carcases shall fall in this wilderness; and all that were numbered of you, according to your whole number, from twenty years old and upward, which have murmured against me,…
Num. 32:11 Surely none of the men that came up out of Egypt, from twenty years old and upward, shall see the land which I sware unto Abraham, unto Isaac, and unto Jacob; because they have not wholly followed me:

The implication is clear- God considered the age of accountability to be twenty years old. If Isaac was twenty years old when Abraham was called to sacrifice him, Isaac was old enough to be accountable in God's eyes. Because Abraham was so faithful to God and had raised his son in the same faith, Isaac did not resist when the knife was lifted against him.

The actions of Abraham and Isaac, up until the angel intervened, foreshadowed the death of the future Messiah. Both Abraham and Isaac were consenting- the actions of a father and a son, both of whom were accountable for their own actions, presents a beautiful type, or foreshadowing, of God the Father offering His only son on our behalf.

Gen 22:14 And Abraham called the name of that place Jehovah-jireh: as it is said to this day, In the mount of the LORD it shall be seen.

400 Years of Exodus 15:13

Gen. 15:13 And he said unto Abram, Know of a surety that thy seed shall be a stranger in a land that is not theirs, and shall serve them; and they shall afflict them four hundred years;.

This 400 years is included in the 430 years discussed earlier. The above Scripture says for 400 years they would be strangers in a land not theirs, they would be subject to or serve the nations in which they dwelled and finally, they would be afflicted. The Scriptures make it plain that all these things happened within the 430 years, of which the 400 years were a part. They would be in a strange land and part of the time they would serve others and even be afflicted. But they were not in slavery the entire time. They were in fact only in Egypt from the time of Joseph in 1706 BC until 1446 BC, or 260 years. They were only enslaved for a few years prior to Moses' birth.

The 430 years includes the entire time Isaac and his descendants were in a foreign land and served others in Canaan and Egypt. They were finally reduced to slavery a little before or about the time Moses was born. They remained in slavery until they were set free at the time of the Exodus. With the date of the Exodus established, the Egyptian Dynasty still had to be determined. The answer to that question came about in an amazing discovery.

The Red Sea Crossing

In 1978, Ron had gone in search of the crossing site of the Red Sea. The accepted location was somewhere along the Gulf of Suez or the Bitter Lakes which formed the eastern boundary of ancient Egypt.

Ron had studied the Biblical story of the Exodus and knew the slaves had to leave the formal border of ancient Egypt the very day they left.

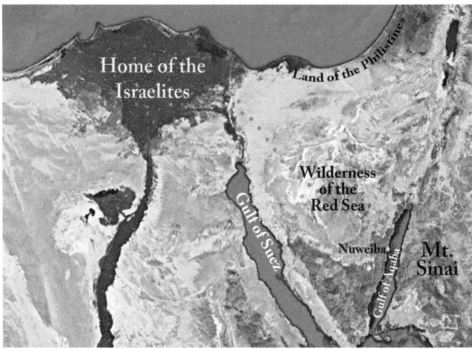

Google Earth

Exo. 13:17 And it came to pass, when Pharaoh had let the people go, that God led them not through the way of the land of the Philistines, although that was near; for God said, Lest peradventure the people repent when they see war, and they return to Egypt: 18 But God led the people about, through the way of the wilderness of the Red sea: and the children of Israel went up harnessed out of the land of Egypt

Google Earth

This understanding would not allow for the crossing to have taken place at the Gulf of Suez or the Bitter lakes. They would still have been inside Egypt proper until they crossed the sea and that conflicts with the Biblical statement.

In order to explore another possibility, he made a search of the western shore of the Gulf of Aqaba. Renting a plane in Eilat, Israel, he first had the pilot fly down the coast as he looked for a possible location for the crossing of the Red Sea. When he saw the large beach of Nuweiba, he then had the plane follow the wadi which exited at the beach to see if it extended through the mountains. Satisfied it did extend completely through, he returned to Nuweiba the next day. Renting scuba gear, Ron and his two sons went diving from the beach at Nuweiba.

On their first dive, they found coral encrusted chariot remains. Being covered in coral made it difficult to see them clearly. The coral was the agent used to preserve them. Any object that old would have long ago dissolved or disintegrated. When the coral attached to them and absorbed the substance of the wheels and axles, the shape of the original object was preserved. The Scriptures tell us why it was reasonable to expect to find these remains:

Exo. 14:24 ...in the morning watch the LORD looked unto the host of the Egyptians through the pillar of fire and of the cloud, and troubled the host of the Egyptians, 25 And took off their chariot wheels, that they drave them heavily:...

They found several six-spoked wheels as well as an eight-spoked wheel. In 1988, Ron found a **four-spoked gold chariot wheel**, which looked almost perfect. The reason this one was so well preserved is because coral does not grow on gold. The wood inside the gold veneer was deteriorated, which made it very fragile. For that reason, he never attempted to retrieve it from the water.

The chariot remains are of extreme importance to the dating of the Exodus and determining which dynasty was involved. A few years later, Ron removed a hub of a wheel from the sea which had the remains of eight spokes radiating outward from it. He realized he was taking a chance because the entire coast of the Gulf of Aqaba is a protected coral area.

Taking it to Cairo, he headed to the office of Dr. Nassif Mohammed Hassan, the Director of Antiquities, with whom Ron had been working. Dr. Hassan immediately stated the specimen was from a chariot of the 18th Dynasty of ancient Egypt. He explained the eight-spoked wheel was only used during the 18th Dynasty. Further research revealed the chariot was relatively new to Egypt at that time:

Mary Nell Lee

One of the first 8 spoked wheels seen by Ron in 1978 off the Nuweiba beach.

Mary Nell Lee

Above and below, the gold wheel Ron found in 1988 using a metal detector.

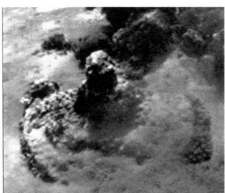

Viveka Pontén

Chariot wheel with part of its axle preserved in coral across from Nuweiba beach in Saudi Arabia. Video by Viveka Pontén who moved to Tabuk, Saudi Arabia to help research for Ron in 1997.

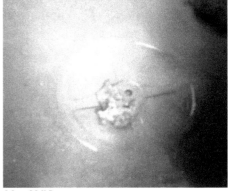

Mary Nell Lee

Below, The shape of an Egyptian sandal in the waters of the Saudi Arabian beach. Also completely consumed by coral, the shape can be seen to be consistent with the depictions to the lower left.

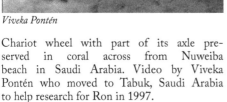

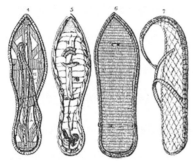

Public Domain

Viveka Pontén

"Egyptian literary references to chariots occur as early as the reigns of Kamose, the 17th Dynasty king who took the first steps in freeing Egypt from the Hyksos, and Ahmose, the founder of the 18th Dynasty. Pictorial representations, however, do not appear until slightly later in the 18th Dynasty...." ("Observations on the Evolving Chariot Wheel in the 18th Dynasty" by James K. Hoffmeier, JARCE #13, 1976).

This indicates it wasn't until the beginning of the 18th Dynasty that the chariot comes into use in the Egyptian army. The Bible mentions during the time of Joseph, chariots were in use since Joseph and his pharaoh drove a chariot, but apparently they weren't developed sturdily enough for use in war until much later.

The author goes on to explain how it was only during the 18th Dynasty that the four, six and eight-spoked wheels were used and monuments can actually be dated by the number of spokes in the wheel:

"Professor Yigael Yadin maintains that during the earlier part of the 18th Dynasty, the Egyptian chariot was `exactly like the Canaanite chariot:' both were constructed of light flexible wood, with leather straps wrapped around the wood to strengthen it, and both utilized wheels with four spokes. In Yadin's eyes, the four-spoked wheel is diagnostic for dating purposes; it is restricted to the early part of the 18th Dynasty. It remained in vogue, he says,

Mary Nell Lee

The beach at Nuweiba, looking southeast where the mountains block any further progress to the south. This is where Ron and his sons, Danny and Ronnie, went diving.

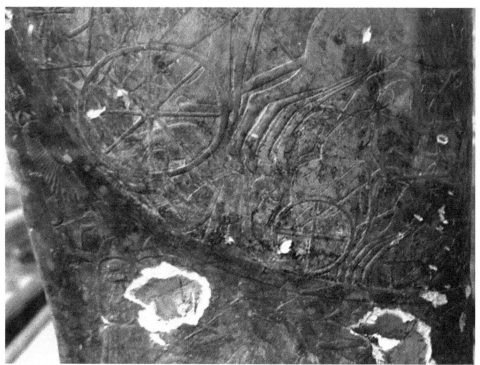

Mary Nell Lee

A damaged chariot cab of 18th Dynasty pharaoh Thutmose IV in the Cairo Museum. In the design on the chariot, the king is driving a chariot with eight-spoked wheels while the enemy soldiers' chariots are depicted with four-spoked wheels.

until the reign of Thutmoses IV, when `the Egyptian chariot begins to shake off its Canaanite influence and undergo considerable change.' Yadin believes that the eight-spoked wheel, which is seen on the body of Thutmoses IV's chariot, was an experiment by the Egyptian wheelwrights, who, when it proved unsuccessful, settled thereafter for the six-spoked wheel. So widespread and meticulous is the delineation of the number of wheel spokes on chariots depicted on Egyptian monuments that they can be used as a criterion for determining whether the monument is earlier or later than 1400 BC." (Hoffmeier).

The Bible tells how the pharaoh took all the chariots of Egypt with him when he chased after the children of Israel:

Exo. 14:6 And he made ready his chariot, and took his people with him: 7 And he took six hundred chosen chariots, and all the chariots of Egypt, and captains over every one of them.

The question Ron had when he found the gold chariot wheel was, "Who would be driving a chariot with gold wheels?" The first thought might be the pharaoh. However, I believe the answer lies in the evidence of the ancient Egyptian and their religion:

"The priests and military men held the highest position in the country after the family of the king, and from them were chosen his ministers and confidential advisers, `the wise counsellors of Pharaoh,' and all the principal officers of state." ("The Ancient Egyptians- Their Life and Customs" by Sir J. Gardner Wilkinson, 1854, vol.1, p.316.)

The priesthood and the military were closely associated. Their system of gods was elaborate and multitudinous. The ultimate god was the one represented as the "Sun." This god was known throughout various times as Amun, Aten and Re or Ra, among other names. All the pharaohs were considered the earthly embodiment of Ra, the origin of the name Rameses.

The divisions of the army were named after the gods, such as *"the first army, that of Amun, the army of Re, the army of Ptah and the army of Sutech."* When they set out to war, elaborate ceremonies were performed at the different temples asking the gods to give them victory over their foes. Then booty gained as a result of their victories was dedicated to the priesthoods

Randall Lee

Viewing Nuweiba from the Arabian beach where the Israelites escaped the army of Egypt. The sun is setting directly over Wadi Watir where the great multitude came through to reach the beach.

and temples of the deities. All military victories were directly attributed to the favor of the gods.

The priests would accompany the army to the battlefield in hopes the gods would show special favor in their battles. Exodus 14:6 strongly implies when pharaoh and his army set out after Moses and the great multitude, he took with him all the priesthood of all the gods of Egypt. During the plagues, he had seen the power of the true God, "I Am" and pharaoh was clearly furious at the death of his son and the Egyptian army needed all the supernatural intervention by the hands of their "so-called gods" as was possible.

This may explain the gold-veneered, four-spoked chariot wheel Ron found in 1988. Since he found it on the Egyptian side of the Gulf of Aqaba, the indication is whoever was driving that particular chariot was at the rear of the army. It seems a valid conclusion that a priest who is not trained in battle would be at the rear of the army. There is an inscription of Thutmose III (18th Dynasty) which relates the Retenu (ancient Egyptian name for Canaanites and Syrians) used gold chariots and were captured as booty by the Egyptians:

"He went forth, none like him, slaying the barbarians, smiting Retenu, bringing their princes as living captives, their chariots wrought with gold, bound to their horses."

There are many inscriptions of the kings of the 18th Dynasty receiving gold-plated foreign chariots, either as spoils of war or as tribute received from conquered peoples. There are also inscriptions telling these gilded chariots were many times dedicated to various temples and gods, which meant the priests would receive these chariots.

There are also inscriptions which describe how the king went to war in a "glittering chariot of electrum" as stated in one of Thutmose III's inscriptions but it is doubtful the pharaoh chasing the multitude would have remained at the rear of the army. Ron concluded the gold wheel most likely belonged to a member of the priestly caste who was accompanying the army, or possibly a high minister of state. We have evidence from ancient tombs that the Egyptians constructed wheels of this design. The Retenu (Cannanite/Syrian) chariot wheels were also of this same design and size.

Ron faced a tremendous amount of resistance concerning the discovery of the chariot wheels since he was not able to bring any to the surface and prove his claims other than the hub he gave to Dr. Hassan. He learned Dr. Hassan had passed away when he went to see him in 1988 and he never found out what happened to the hub he had taken to him.

Mount Sinai in Saudi Arabia

Rather than enter into controversy with anyone as to what they saw, it is enough to say that it convinced Ron. His belief was strong enough to convince him, without a doubt, Mount Sinai was across the Gulf of Aqaba in Saudi Arabia. This belief cost him and his sons 78 days in a Saudi prison in 1984 after entering the country illegally. But that trip paid off because he found the holy mountain of God and today it is widely accepted that Jebel el Maqla in the Jebel el Lawz range is the true Mount Sinai. This is covered in detail in chapter 18.

It also convinced him the 18th Dynasty, without a doubt, was the time of the Exodus. Once he had this firm conviction, he was able to examine the evidence with confidence.

Chapter 3

Egypt Before the Exodus

To get a complete picture of anything, information has to be presented in its proper context. It has been extremely difficult to piece together the data for this subject due to all the data being presented in a theoretical context in every paper and book I have studied. Since the beginning of the science of archaeology, the person or persons who make a discovery are the ones who determined how the evidence is interpreted. If there is a disagreement, the loudest and most influential voice usually wins out as in the case of Jericho in chapter 19. Also, the only accepted data must come from within the closed group of scholars on each subject.

Egypt is a unique country. The Nile River flows northward and exits into the Mediterranean Sea on Egypt's northern border. The fertile regions of the country are the Delta region and the land along the river. Vast areas of desert are not inhabited even today. In order for land outside of a water source to be livable, water must be somehow brought in. This resulted in Egypt's population being situated along the Nile and in the Delta along the Nile branches.

Many people assume the pharaoh of the Exodus was named Rameses which was a name for pharaohs in the 19th and 20th Dynasties. Yet, the name "Rameses" is mentioned in the Bible as early as the story of Joseph.

An understanding of their religion shows how it was more a title than a name, much like the title "pharaoh." "Pharaoh" means "great house," not king, even though it later came to be used to designate the ruler. Egyptian records show every native Egyptian king from early times was considered the "Son of the Sun" or "Rameses." The Biblical reference to the name Rameses is simply indicative of the fact that it was land that belonged to the ruler who was the "Son of the Sun."

Ancient historians listed the kings of Egypt in a continuous line, one after the other, as did the various King's lists that have been preserved. This resulted

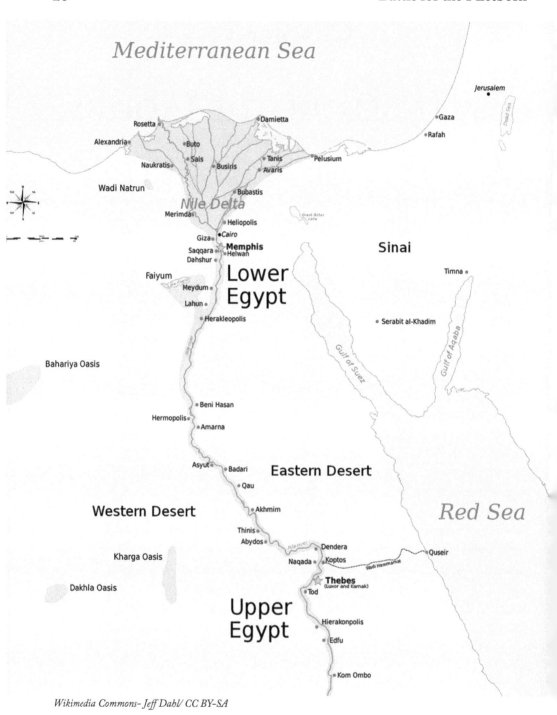

Ancient Egypt's population was completely concentrated along the Nile River and the lush Delta area, which was the home of the Israelites. The main part of the country is desert with no water source and incompatible with life except where rarely a spring may be found.

in a number of years of reigns that were not realistic nor even possible. It is apparent that due to the layout of Egypt, with vast distances between the major settled areas, different families formed their own family dynasties and ruled independently in their own regions. Historical records don't show any real conflicts between the native families.

All left bits and pieces of their history in statues and inscriptions in stone. But without a real calendar, it is impossible to date anything. To accurately date anything you must have a reference point. We resolved that issue to a degree with the solid date of the Exodus based on the Biblical statement which gave us a point of reference.

Another problem for the scholar is that the ancient Egyptians recorded all events in a way that made them look righteous, powerful and successful. They were masters of propaganda.

When we realize that the ancient Egyptians were very superstitious and had a multitude of gods they had to honor and placate, some things begin to fall into place. Almost all inscriptions are found in temples and tombs proving they are directed to the gods, not to the normal person. Most of the common people were illiterate.

In the 18th Dynasty, the pharaoh was the complete and absolute ruler. He still owned all the land, something that began when Joseph's pharaoh bought all the land from the people because of the famine. He was actually viewed as a god. He had advisors and officials to handle all phases of the government but he was the final word on all decisions.

The ancient Egyptian religion was involved in all facets of the Egyptian's life. The Egyptian king was considered the earthly embodiment of the god; which god depended upon the gods his family venerated the most and varied by location. Ra was always considered a major god and one of the names the king would take.

Their beliefs in the afterlife provided virtual control over the people who feared being cast into eternal darkness if they didn't comply with the wishes of the gods and the king. This was a perfect mode of controlling the population. Death rituals and spells of the priests made them powerful and kept the people under control of the throne.

To undertake a study of any ancient people, many things must also be considered such as their religious beliefs. The nature of the country is important as well, such as the layout of Egypt which caused the native population to be spread out over a long, narrow area. This made unity of the nation much more difficult and also resulted in different dynasties ruling contemporaneously throughout the nation.

Organization into Dynasties

The division into dynasties is an artificial separation devised by Manetho of the 3rd century BC but is useful for purposes of organization. The 17th Dynasty was a family who lived in Thebes, the southern capitol and the 18th Dynasty was a continuation of that same family.

First Mention of Egypt in the Bible

Egypt was settled early in history although the exact time cannot be known. The first mention of Egypt in the Bible is in Genesis 12:1 when Abraham, then called Abram, went into Egypt during a famine. Since Abram was 75 years old when he left Haran and went to Canaan, it is reasonable to say Egypt was firmly established by 1921 BC, just 427 years after the flood. Soon after his arrival in Canaan, he and his wife Sarai went to Egypt because of a famine.

The Biblical account is extremely short on the subject of Abram's visit to Egypt but we learn Abram misled the pharaoh. The pharaoh, because of Sarai's beauty, took her to his palace as one of his wives. Out of fear, Abram told him she was his sister which was partially true since she was his half-sister, but she was also his wife. The king paid Abram well for Sarai but God intervened, causing plagues of an unknown type to fall upon the pharaoh and the country. When the pharaoh figured out the cause for these pestilences, he called Abram and asked him why he lied to him about Sarai. Then Abram and his entourage were escorted out of Egypt.

Egypt was already a rich nation and it was at this time Abram became rich in cattle, gold and silver, given to him as payment for Sarai as no mention is made of the pharaoh asking him to return all he was given.

Josephus wrote that Abraham was responsible for bringing the knowledge of arithmetic and astronomy to the Egyptians, which may also be true since he came from the land of the Chaldees which was rich in scientific knowledge.

The time of Abram's visit to Egypt was probably early in the 1st Dynasty and there is good reason to believe it was at this time that the regulation prohibiting the Egyptians from eating, drinking or fraternizing with foreign shepherds was instituted (Gen. 46:34).

The next mention of Egypt comes from the time of Joseph which will be covered in great detail in chapter 4.

The Golden Calf

When the children of Israel left Egypt and finally arrived at Mount Sinai, they had a golden calf made in Moses' absence while he was receiving the Ten Commandments from God. In Egypt, there were two cow gods that had been venerated since the early days of Egypt's establishment- Hathor and Apis.

Hathor was the daughter of Ra, the creator sun god. She was the goddess of love, motherhood, fertility and much more. It is difficult to identify exactly her position as a goddess except to say that she was deeply revered and identified with the royal house. There are statues of Hathor as a cow goddess with the disc of Ra between her horns.

The male bull god, Apis, was worshiped and considered to be god living on the earth. There was a festival held in Memphis where the sacred bull was led through the streets by the priests. On the death of the Apis bull, he was embalmed and buried with great care.

Either of these Egyptian bovine gods could have been the origination of the golden calf. At the foot of Mount Sinai in Saudi Arabia is a very large altar-like structure which is covered with pictures of bulls and cows in the Egyptian style of Hathor and Apis.

Mary Nell Lee

Left- Hathor.

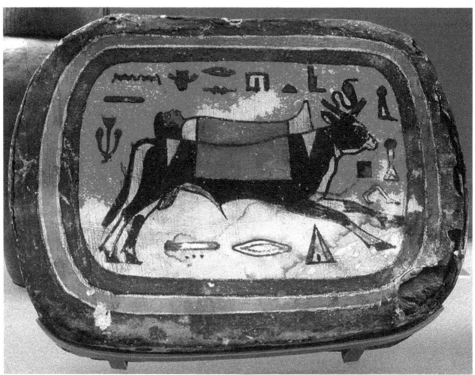

Mary Nell Lee

Randall Lee   **Above**– two depictions of the bull god, Apis.

Viveka Pontén

Above is a large arrangement of rocks in Saudi Arabia about one kilometer from the base of Jebel Maqla, the mountain Ron believed was Mount Sinai. This large grouping of rocks contains a large number of etchings of cows and bulls. These resemble drawings of Hathor and Apis in ancient Egyptian tombs and monuments.

It is believed to be the site of the golden calf altar of the Biblical account. Today, the Saudi Arabia government has enclosed the site in a chain link fence and posted signs stating that it is designated as an archaeological site.

Randall Lee

Randall Lee

Above are two of the many cow and bull petroglyphs on the altar site in Saudi Arabia. The top image resembles the Apis bull while the bottom image has horns in the configuration of Hathor.

Chapter 4

JOSEPH

The Biblical account of Joseph must be accepted as true if we are going to rely on the Scriptures as our guide. Going that far back into history is difficult since Egypt had no calendar with which to provide dating. But there is definitely information which must be considered.

Joseph's family was a Semitic-speaking family who lived in Canaan. There was no Jewish designation at that time; they were called Hebrews. Joseph, in Gen. 40:15, says he was "stolen away out of the land of the Hebrews," referring to his being sold by his brothers to a band of Midianites while in the land of Canaan. The story of Joseph is vital to the subject of the Exodus and it can be found in Genesis chapters 30 through 50.

In the 3rd Dynasty, there appeared on the scene an incredible individual in the ancient records by the name of Imhotep. Manetho wrote

"During his [Djoser of the 3rd Dynasty] reign lived Imouthes [i.e., Imhotep], who, because of his medical skill has the reputation of Asclepius [the Greek god of medicine] among the Egyptians and who was the inventor of the art of building with hewn stone."

It was this statement that caused the scholars to doubt the existence of a real person named Imhotep. But in 1926, the question was settled once and for all. When excavations were carried out at the Step Pyramid at Saqqara, fragments of a statue of Pharaoh Djoser were found. The base was inscribed with the names of Djoser and the name of his second in command:

"Imhotep, Chancellor of the King of Lower Egypt, Chief under the King, Administrator of the Great Palace, Hereditary Lord, High Priest of Heliopolis, Imhotep the Builder, the Sculptor, the Maker of Stone Vases...".

Mary Nell Lee
Pharaoh Djoser of the 3rd Dynasty at Saqqara.

Gen. 41:40 Thou shalt be over my house, and according unto thy word shall all my people be ruled: only in the throne will I be greater than thou.... 43 And he made him to ride in the second chariot which he had; and they cried before him, Bow the knee: and he made him ruler over all the land of Egypt. 44 And Pharaoh said unto Joseph, I am Pharaoh, and without thee shall no man lift up his hand or foot in all the land of Egypt.

Joseph's position under the pharaoh was that of a prime minister, among many other titles, and Imhotep appears to have been the first who held such a vast range of authority in ancient Egypt.

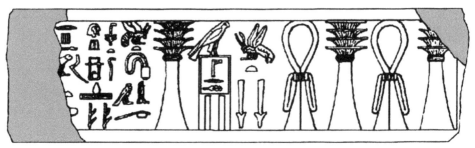

Wikimedia Commons- GDK/ CC BY-SA
The pedestal of Pharaoh Djoser of the 3rd Dynasty with the titles of Imhotep.

The "Famine Stele".

The Famine Stele

The evidence which connects Imhotep with Joseph is an amazing inscription found carved on a large rock on the island of Sihel just below the First Cataract of the Nile. This inscription claims to be a copy of a document written by Djoser in the 18th year of his reign. Written over 1,000 years after the events it claims to be relating, it goes on to tell of a seven years of plenty and seven years of famine. The story was corrupted over time but it shows that in the collective memory of the ancient Egyptians, the story was still believed to be true.

The inscription recorded Djoser's promise to the Nile god, Khnum, in which the people were to be taxed 1/10 of everything, except for the priests of the house of the god, who would be exempted. This fact is corrupted but still obviously had the same ancient origin as the Biblical story of Joseph.

Gen. 47:26 And Joseph made it a law over the land of Egypt unto this day, that Pharaoh should have the fifth part, except the land of the priests only, which became not Pharaoh's.

A similar inscription was found on the Isle of Philae. However that one has the priests of Isis stating that Djoser made the same gift to their god for the same purpose. Just as the story of the flood is found in almost every ancient culture but is twisted to fit their own purposes and gods, here we find the story of Joseph. In this case the story is also twisted to fit the needs of the priests of the various gods in substantiating their claims to certain land.

All of the major components of the Biblical account are present in these inscriptions, except that the story has been Egyptianized with their ancient gods.

It is believed that this inscription was written during the 2nd century BC by the priests of Khnum for the purpose of justifying their claim of some land privileges. Part of the inscription states that the pharaoh dedicated some of the land and taxation to the god.

There is more compelling evidence for the story of Joseph in Saqqara. An examination of Egyptian history reveals it was during the time of Djoser that Egypt, for the first time, became an exceptionally powerful nation. The reason for that can be found in the story of Joseph.

Randall Lee
The Step Pyramid of Pharaoh Djoser built by Imhotep.

Imhotep- Builder of 1st Pyramid

Imhotep is known as the architect of the 1st pyramid in all of Egypt. This alone is enough to have made him famous. But there is evidence of something much more important.

During the 7seven years of plenty, under Joseph's wise guidance, the pharaoh began to organize a well run administrative center which handled the selling of the grain to all the surrounding nations. During the famine, Egypt had gathered the wealth of all the surrounding nations by selling them grain.

Evidence of this historic event can be found in Saqqara at the Step Pyramid complex of Pharaoh Djoser. A large complex was built which surrounded the future burial site of the pharaoh within this pyramid.

The Step Pyramid complex at Saqqara

The complex is surrounded by a huge wall. Within this complex is the Step Pyramid which was the 1st pyramid ever built in Egypt. At the main entrance on the east wall, at the southern end, is the entry into a long hall of 40 columns, 20 on each side. Each column is connected to the main wall by a perpendicular wall, forming small cubicles between each column.

As this colonnade is exited, straight ahead is a series of very deep bins. These are extremely large in size, much larger than any burial chambers and they are all centrally accessible by connecting chutes.

In addition, these massive pits extend several feet above ground level, which indicates that they were not hidden, as were tombs. Because the ancient Egyptians buried their dead with so much valuable material and provisions for their afterlife, plundering of tombs was always their biggest fear. Therefore, it is apparent that these massive bins had another purpose.

In all the other ancient cities, whenever large bins such as these were uncovered by archaeologists, they were recognized as grain storage bins. The evidence is compelling that these were huge bins used to contain massive amounts of grain.

Additional evidence is found in Djoser's burial complex under the Step Pyramid. Within his tomb are smaller matching bins for the king and his family's afterlife and in these bins were found grain and other food stuffs.

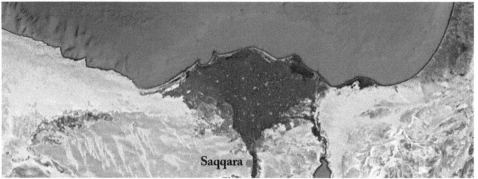

Google Earth

Reconstruction of
The STEP PYRAMID Complex

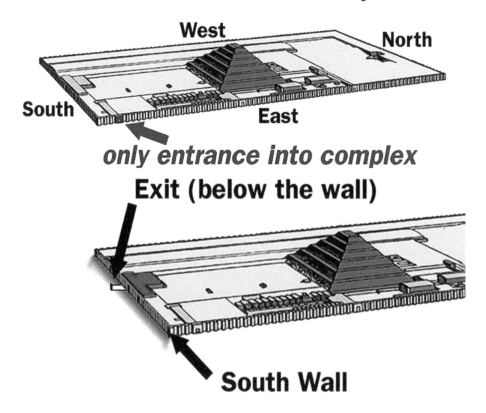

All of the grain bins are located in the red area in the above diagram. The only exit can also be seen above. After purchasing grain, the buyer would then descend a long stairway which would lead them outside of the wall. The location was convenient for people coming from Canaan and countries to the east and north. It was also convenient for anyone coming from the west or by water via the Mediterranean Sea.

In the Biblical account, we learn that Joseph appointed men throughout the land of Egypt to oversee the gathering and storing of the grain in all the cities:

Gen. 41:34 Let Pharaoh do this, and let him appoint officers over the land, and take up the fifth part of the land of Egypt in the seven plenteous years. 35 And let them gather all the food of those good years that come, and lay up corn under the hand of Pharaoh, and let them keep food in the cities.

Joseph had given this plan to the pharaoh prior to his appointment as vizier or prime minister. Since it would have been impossible for him to oversee the gathering and storing of grain for the entire country, he had implemented a plan with provisions for gathering grain from the whole of Egypt.

This meant the organization of a large force of trustworthy and capable men. When the famine began and the Egyptians began to cry for food, they were told to go to Joseph and do whatever he said, which indicates that he personally gave the orders for the distribution of the grain:

Gen. 41:55 And when all the land of Egypt was famished, the people cried to Pharaoh for bread: and Pharaoh said unto all the Egyptians, Go unto Joseph; what he saith to you, do. 56 And the famine was over all the face of the earth: and Joseph opened all the storehouses, and sold unto the Egyptians; and the famine waxed sore in the land of Egypt.

When foreign peoples came to purchase grain, they also went directly to Joseph:

Gen. 42:6 And Joseph was the governor over the land, and he it was that sold to all the people of the land: and Joseph's brethren came, and bowed down themselves before him with their faces to the earth.

The complex at Saqqara is unique and nothing like it has ever been found. It was described by William Hayes as being a:

"...veritable city in itself, planned and executed as a single unit and built of fine white limestone from the nearby Mukattam Hills." ("The Scepter of Egypt, Vol. 1," p. 60.)

Ron believed without question that this was the central location of the grain bins which stored the grain for the famine.

Randall Lee

The only entrance into the Step Pyramid Complex.

Randall Lee

The long corridor which exits into the south end of the Step Pyramid complex. There are 20 columns on each side across from each other. No statues were found in these spaces which indicates they had another purpose. Ron believed they were the perfect size for clerks to sit and help with the buying of the grain.

The step pyramid complex was conveniently located for the other nations who came to obtain their grain. This is a major consideration which needs to be understood in order to meet the qualifications for being a major center of commerce related to the selling of the grain to all the foreign nations.

During the seven year famine, Egypt gained great wealth and prominence among the nations through the selling of the grain. The Egyptians who lived in their cities along the Nile had little to do during the famine since they had a seven year supply of grain to rely on. As a result, they were able to devote their time to the building projects of the pharaoh, not as slaves, but as grateful subjects.

Finally, in gratitude to Joseph, the pharaoh granted to Joseph's family the right to live in the land of Goshen:

Gen 47:27 And Israel dwelt in the land of Egypt, in the country of Goshen; and they had possessions therein, and grew, and multiplied exceedingly. (Also called the land of Rameses in Gen. 47:11.)

Just as God had provided great wealth to Abram which allowed him to settle his family in Canaan comfortably, God provided a safe haven for the family of Jacob, who was later named Israel by God. The children of Israel grew and thrived, unmolested by the Egyptian population. As most ancient remains have crumbled and been damaged greatly, the complex at the Step Pyramid remained intact enough to provide the evidence of what took place there.

Joseph, who lived to be 110, lived through the reign of numerous other pharaohs and perhaps served under them as well. When he died, he was embalmed and placed in a casket. But before he died, he reminded his people that they were still strangers in Egypt and one day they would leave:

Gen. 50:25 And Joseph took an oath of the children of Israel, saying, God will surely visit you, and ye shall carry up my bones from hence.

From the time Jacob's family came to Egypt until the birth of Moses was about 180 years. Many pharaohs had come and gone, many ruling contemporaneously with others in different regions. For many years, all the pharaohs recognized the rights granted to the people of Israel to live in the land of Rameses. But that would one day change.

Randall Lee

A niche between two columns in the long colonnade entranceway into the complex. These are the perfect size for a person to set with a table and handle the transactions for the buying of grain. There are enough to have people who speak the different languages of the region.

Randall Lee

The pyramid can be seen by looking to the right after entering the complex through the colonnade.

Mary Nell Lee
Ron is walking by the largest bin. The others have remnants of the familiar "grain bin" curved top.

Simplified diagram of basic design.
Not to scale; placement not precise.

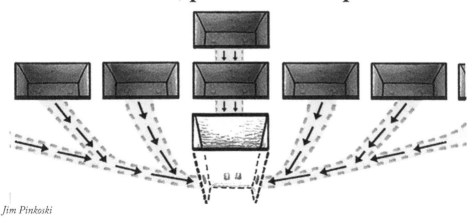

Jim Pinkoski

All the bins are connected by chutes. As one of the bins being used began to get low on grain, the chute was opened and it was refilled.

Randall Lee

Above- the large open bin seen soon after entering the complex.
Top right- the chute can be partially seen.
Bottom right- Viewing the complex from outside the wall, the top of the colonnade can be seen mid-right. The familiar "grain bin" shape can be seen to the left of that.

to "chute"

Mary Nell Lee

From a Theban Tomb (Wilkinson)

Mary Nell Lee

Randall Lee

Stairway leading to the exit outside the wall. This was necessary as there was only one entrance and this ensured a smooth operation as grain was obtained.

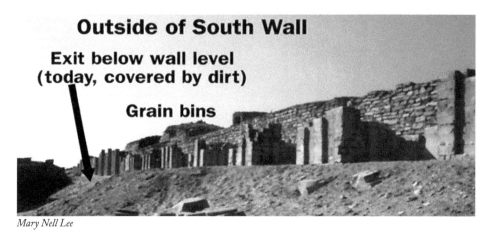

Mary Nell Lee

Chapter 5

THE HYKSOS

The Merneptah Stele in the Cairo Museum. Telling of 19th Dynasty pharaoh Merneptah's military victories, the next to the last line is translated: "Israel is laid waste and his seed is not." This translation is debated among scholars.

There are no inscriptions found which mention the children of Israel being in Egypt. The only mention of Israel is on the Stele of Merneptah who was the fourth pharaoh of the 19th Dynasty. The date of this stele is also after the time of the Exodus and is not universally accepted by scholars.

But there is ample documentation that there were foreign people who came into the Delta region called the "Hyksos," a mixed Semitic-speaking people. The Hyksos were very important to the events leading up to the Exodus. It is generally accepted that the Hyksos were also Hebrews since they were Semites.

But the Hyksos were not the Israelites. They were people who came to settle in the land given to Jacob's family which was an extremely large area. The impact they had on Egypt was one of great progress in many arenas.

Their very presence in the Delta is an indirect proof that the Israelites were there as well. It makes sense that Jacob's family welcomed others from their home in Canaan to settle alongside of them due to the vast amount of land there and the available water supply. But the Hyksos were not worshippers of the true God and the children of Israel remained separate from them.

The Hyksos grew in size and in power, eventually harassing native dynastic families. They formed their own dynasties, had their own gods and brought technical knowledge to Egypt as well as new breeds of animals such as horses. They first introduced the horse and chariot as a war machine and advanced weaponry.

Their capital was Avaris in the Egyptian Delta about 40 miles northeast of Cairo. Excavations have been carried on there since the 1960's by Austrian archaeologist, Manfred Bietak. His excavations have revealed that the city was a major capital for the trading of imported goods due to its access to the Mediterranean Sea via the Nile branches. Temples were not dedicated to the Egyptian gods but instead to the storm gods of Syria, such as Baal Zephon.

The city was large, estimated to have a population of approximately 25,000 people. They carried on diplomatic relationships with foreign nations. They introduced glass-making to Egypt along with other technologies.

There has been a great deal written about the Hyksos, much of it painting them as marauders who invaded Egypt and took it over by force. But the truth appears to be quite different.

The Egyptian historian, Manetho, is the one who first portrayed them in such a dark light. Instead, the evidence paints a picture of a people who brought great knowledge to Egypt which helped them later attain their status as the greatest world empire by the 18th Dynasty.

The decision was soon made that the Hyksos needed to be eliminated

Painting on the wall of the tomb of Khnumhotep III at Beni Hasan showing Asiatics coming to Egypt with either gifts, items to trade, or items they would use if they settled there.

from the country. The true reason is not really known but there is a petty story recorded in the Sallier Papyrus I about the Hyksos King, Apepi, and the Egyptian king, Seqenenre:

It happened that the land of Egypt belonged to the Impure, and as there was no lord monarch that day, it happened then that the king Soqnun-rî was sovereign over the country of the South, and that the Impure of the city of Ra were subject to Ra-Apôpi in Hâuâru; the entire country paid him tribute together with its manufactured products and so loaded him with all the good things of To-miri.

Now the king Ra-Apôpi took the god Sutekhu for his master, and he no longer served any (other) deity who was in the whole country excepting only Sutekhu, and he built a temple of excellent and imperishable workmanship at the gate of the king Ra-Apôpi, and he arose each day to sacrifice daily victims to Sutekhu; and the vassal chiefs of the sovereign were there with garlands of flowers, just as is the case in the temple of Ph-Ra-Har-ma-khuti.

And the king Ra-Apôpi bethought himself of sending a message to announce it to the king Soqnun-rî, the prince of the city of the South. And many days after that, the king Ra-Apôpi summoned his great chiefs, as well as his captains and his prudent generals, but they could not suggest to him a speech which was good to send to the king Soqnun-rî the chief of the country of the South. So the king Apôpi summoned his scribes versed in magic. They said to him: "O suzerain, our master," and they suggested to the king Ra-Apôpi the discourse which he desired: Let a messenger go to the chief of the city of the South and say to him: The king Ra-Apôpi sends to say: Let the hippopotamuses which are in the canals of the country be chased on the pool, in order that they may allow sleep to visit me night and day...."

He will not know what to answer, whether good or bad: then thou shalt send him another message: "The king Ra-Apôpi sends saying: If the chief of the South cannot answer my message, let him serve no other god than Sutekhu! But if he answers it, and does that which I bid him do, then I will take nothing from him, and I will no more bow down before any other god of the land of Egypt except Amon-Ra the king of the gods!"

And many days after that, the king Ra-Apôpi sent to the prince of the country of the South the message which his scribes versed in magic had suggested to him; and the messenger of the king Ra-Apôpi came to the chief of the land of the South. He said to the messenger of the king Ra-Apôpi: "What message dost thou bring to the land of the South? Why hast thou made this journey?"

The messenger replied: "The king Ra-Apôpi sends to say: Let the hippopotamuses which are in the canals of the country be chased on the pool, in order that they may allow sleep to visit me day and night.…"

The chief of the land of the South was astounded and knew not what answer to make to the messenger of the king Ra-Apôpi. So the chief of the land of the South said to the messenger: "This is what thy master sends to … the chief of the land of the South … the words which he has sent me … his goods.…"

The chief of the land of the South caused all kinds of good things, meats, cakes, … (and) wine to be given to the messenger; then he said to him: "Return and tell thy master … all that which thou hast said, I approve.…"

The messenger of the king Ra-Apôpi set himself to return to the place where his master was. Then the chief of the South summoned his great chiefs as well as his captains and his able generals, and he repeated to them all the message which the king Ra-Apôpi had sent to him. Then they were silent with a single mouth for a long moment (of time), and did not know what answer to make whether good or bad.

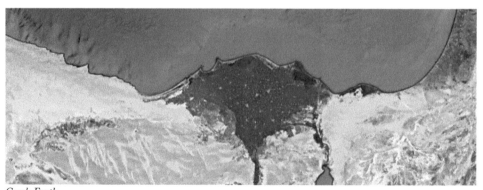

Goggle Earth

The Delta area of Egypt can be seen clearly in this satellite image.

The king Ra-Apôpi sent to the chief of the land of the South the other message which his scribes versed in magic had suggested to him....

And it ended there- the papyrus was damaged, or perhaps it wasn't completed, but we have a general idea of what happened next. Historic data says that the 17th dynasty ruled in Thebes, in the south of Egypt, while a Hyksos dynasty ruled in Avaris in the north, considered to be the 15th Dynasty.

The Hyksos pharaoh, Apepi, usurped the monuments of earlier pharaohs and placed his name on them and eventually began to harrass the Theban king, culminating in the message related in the Sallier Papyrus I.

We don't have access to any earlier interactions between these two rulers but it appears this was the last straw for the 17th Dynasty Theban king, Seqenenre Tao. He went to war with the northern pharaoh and he lost the battle.

The mummy of Pharaoh Seqenenre shows gruesome head wounds. Comparisons of his wounds to Hyksos battle axes have been made and determined to prove his injuries were the result of such a war instrument.

Seqenenre was not properly prepared for burial which points to his being killed in battle. Although mummified, his body reveals the gruesome and fatal wounds.

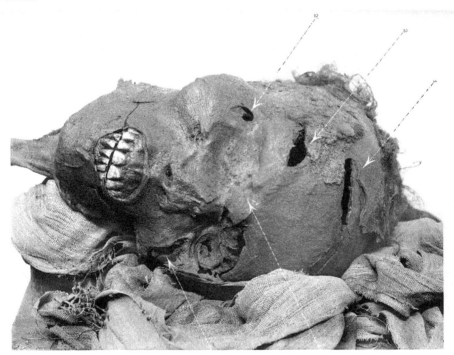

Gaston Maspero/ Public Domain
The head of the mummy of Seqenenre Tao.

Wikimedia Commons- Jeff Dahl/ CC BY-SA

Seqenenre's son, Kamose, continued the battle with Apepi but also didn't succeed in winning the war. Finally Kamose's brother, Ahmose, completed the war and expelled the Hyksos from Egypt. These Semitic people were routed out of the country and returned to Canaan, Syria and Lebanon where they had originally lived.

The Rhind Papyrus gives an account of Ahmose's military strategy. The Hyksos capitol was Avaris in the Nile Delta. Strategically, instead of attacking Avaris, he took Heliopolis and then took Tjaru, the major border fortress on the road from Egypt to Canaan. By capturing Tjaru, he blocked the passageway between Canaan and Avaris. This blockade prevented them from obtaining supplies or military help.

The tomb walls of Ahmose, the son of Ebana, gives further information. Ahmose led three attacks against Avaris, the Hyksos capital, but also had a small rebellion arise further south in Egypt which took his attention. Finally in his fourth attack against Avaris, he was victorious.

After a three year siege, he conquered their stronghold near Gaza, Sharuhen. Many years after he completed his expulsion, in his regnal year 22, an inscription relating to the opening of the quarry at Tura stated that "oxen from Canaan" were used. This was most likely tribute obtained from the expelled Hyksos. He then continued his military campaigns in Syria and Nubia.

Pharaoh Ahmose then became the first pharaoh of the 18th Dynasty. Ruling from Thebes, he had conquered and expelled the people who had taken control of Northern Egypt. The stage was set and things were about to happen for the children of Israel.

Chapter 6

18TH DYNASTY RECONSTRUCTION

This reconstruction of the 18th Dynasty is radical but when assembled in a timeline, the timing is consistent with the events of the Exodus. When Ron told me his theory that the 18th Dynasty was the time of the Exodus, I was perplexed when I looked at the available data about the various personalities involved.

New Theory

He then told me one thing that changed everything: he said that **some of the different pharaohs were actually the same person in a different capacity.** As he studied the Kings Lists of ancient Egypt, he was struck by the fact that their names appeared in a line of alternating similar names. He concluded that in the 18th Dynasty, the Thutmoses and Amenhoteps were not separate individuals but the same king ruling first as the co-regent, then later as the emperor.

I searched for the earliest records on each subject and aspect of the 18th Dynasty. Thankfully, I lived near universities and libraries where I could access a great deal of the early archaeological journals that recorded all the discoveries at the time they were made. I wrote to various archaeologists asking for information when I couldn't find information for which I was looking. This was well before the availability of so much data on the Internet. I began to compose a chronological timeline using all the dates we are given from monuments, statues, temples, foundation deposits and tomb inscriptions for all the different people in the dynasty. Adjusting the events of the particular Thutmose with the appropriate Amenhotep, I looked for overlapping events that would confirm this theory was a possibility.

As I read and devoured all the oldest data available, a picture began to form of how different people within the dynasty were placed in their historical perspective long ago during the earliest phases of the new science of archaeology. As new information came from more recent discoveries, the die had already been cast and the original beliefs continued to be accepted. There is an overwhelming amount of data available but scholars and Egyptologists cannot agree on the overall picture. Papers have been written by brilliant men and women, promoting an abundance of beliefs on how the dynasty fit together but none of it provides a complete chronology. There are statements constantly found about the difficulties in explaining different issues.

As the known dates for different people were pieced together, I discovered a totally different picture than is generally presented and accepted. With this one correction, the evidence fit into the Exodus model perfectly! It must be remembered that all ancient archaeological conclusions are circumstantial when there is not a reliable calendar to use. The ancient Egyptians had no such calendar and everything on their monuments, walls and papyri were dated to the year of the reigning monarch.

Separating data from theory was difficult. Sometimes, when there is not a date known for the death of a particular pharaoh, the general practice seems to have been to place his death at or near his last dated monument. There are times when I believe the evidence indicates some pharaohs lived longer than is commonly accepted.

Events Prior to the Exodus Importance

It was vital to find events that could have logically applied to the Exodus story prior to it happening. The first major point was determining at the beginning of this dynasty, the expulsion of the Hyksos from the Nile Delta region occurred very near where the children of Israel were already granted to live in the land of Goshen.

The 18th Dynasty left a massive amount of monuments, complexes, mortuary temples, statues and evidences that proved it became supremely wealthy, organized and a world power. How was this possible in such a short time? The innovations learned from the Hyksos brought their technology to a new level. They now had abilities they never had before. They were able to provide their army with the latest technical advances such as the strong war chariot. They had a slave labor force in the Israelites that must have included many talented artists of all kinds who most certainly did more than make mud-bricks as the artistry of this dynasty exploded in a mass of exquisite statuary and art of all kinds.

Alternating Names of the Pharaohs

In the 18th Dynasty, there was a series a kings with the names of Amenhotep and Thutmose, each followed by a number to distinguish to which one was being referred. To cut down on confusion, I will only use those commonly known names. Also, the number after the name is not part of their actual name. It is a designation used by scholars to provide an easy reference to each particular king.

There is a very important point to be discussed at this juncture- the alternating names of Amenhotep and Thutmose among the pharaohs who were first co-regent then emperor pharaoh.

Prior to the conquest and expulsion of the Hyksos, the Theban pharaohs had no co-regent. The emperor ruled alone in Thebes. After the nation was unified under the 18th dynasty pharaoh, Ahmose, the need arose for a co-regent to rule in the north.

When Ahmose appointed his son as the first co-regent, he gave his son the royal name of "Amenhotep" to honor Amun. Amun, the chief god of Thebes, was considered the self-created king of all the gods. There can be no question as to why this god was chosen by Ahmose for his son's name when he appointed him as his co-regent. Their name did more than honor the god- they were considered to be the earthly embodiment of that god.

However, when Amenhotep I became senior pharaoh in Thebes after his father Ahmose died, he needed a new name for the position as emperor. He chose Thutmose I in honor of the god Toth. Toth was the main god of Hermopolis, the Biblical city of "On," a part of today's Memphis.

He most likely became a adherent of Toth while he ruled in Memphis. Toth was the god of knowledge, known as the inventor of writing and languages, creator of science, magic, arts, philosophy and the recorder of the records at judgment. He was known for his mediation abilities and justice. Known also as the moon god, he was the source of all knowledge of astronomy and the regulation of times and seasons.

When Amenhotep I became the emperor pharaoh Thutmose I and moved to Thebes, he had to appoint a co-regent who would rule in Memphis. He chose a name for his co-regent that honored the god, Toth and reserved the Amenhotep name for the senior pharaoh in Thebes. This meant that after Thutmose I, following pharaohs would have a "Thutmose" name as co-regent in Memphis and an "Amenhotep" name as emperor pharaoh ruling in Thebes. The pharaoh was the embodiment of the main god of the city in which he ruled.

Developing the Timeline

It took a number of years to complete the timeline about to be presented. The main reason was the difficulty of finding the pure data revealed in the ancient records. Almost everything has been presented in the context of theory which is presented as fact without providing the original data. I only wanted the data without the conclusions.

As I collected data of various accomplishments and dates of each pharaoh, I began to overlay them with each other. If king "X" was also king "Y", I needed to be sure there weren't any problems and that the data could provide the correlation between the two kings.

In the timeline on the following pages, each pharaoh who is the same person as both a co-regent and a senior pharaoh are presented in the same color.

I also want to stress that the lists of Manetho and other ancient writers cannot be relied upon. They have listed all the kings down through Egyptian history in a linear pattern, one after the other. Yet, it is known that many kings ruled contemporaneously with each other. In the early years of ancient Egypt, the vastness of the country allowed for different rulers to arise in different regions. They would rule over their own immediate area without any evidence of infighting among others in different areas.

I will present only major facts of each pharaoh and show relevant issues. The charts that I constructed to confirm that the different pharaohs were actually the same people are too involved to present in this book. I attempted to use only information that simplifies the chain of events.

A major issue was a number of dated monuments which give only a regnal year but not the name of the pharaoh. Those will be discussed in the chapters ahead.

Timeline of Moses' Life

The Biblical story of the Exodus is built around the 80 years of Moses' life:

- The first 40 years concern Moses' life in Egypt.
- The next 40 years concern events that occurred in Egypt while he was in Midian.
- In the 80th year, Moses returned to Egypt at the command of God to demand that the pharaoh let the Israelites go into the wilderness 3 days to worship their God. They were then supposed to return to Egypt.

- When the pharaoh finally let them go, they didn't return after three days. They instead continued their journey at the command of God to the mountain where God had spoken to Moses, Mount Sinai in Midian.

This timeline includes an 80 year span beginning with the birth of Moses and concludes with Moses' 80th year when the Exodus occurs. It begins a few years prior to Moses birth and concludes with the Exodus.

Events After the Exodus

The events in Egypt after the Exodus are extremely difficult to accurately date in a timeline due to the dearth of records. However, there is a great deal of evidence allowing us to know basically what transpired and the general time span. This book continues to document events after the Exodus until the time of the Israelites entry into Canaan even though they cannot be dated with complete accuracy.

How to Read the Chronological Timeline

- The chart begins with Moses' age in the left column in the color purple.
- All dates in ancient Egypt on monuments, inscriptions and other items are given as the year of the reign of the pharaoh.
- Each pharaoh is shown in a column with his regnal years.
- Pharaohs who are the same person with two different names as shown in columns side by side in the same color.
- For example, Amenhotep I and Thutmose I are the same person and therefore placed side by side in the same color. This person has two different lists of regnal years, one in his name of Amenhotep I when he was co-regent, and another in his name of Thutmose I when he was emperor pharaoh. Something dated in "year 13" of Amenhotep I is the same as "year 1" in his reign as Thutmose I. It is crucial to keep this concept in mind. Most pharaohs have two separate lists of regnal years.
- The years of Hatshepsut are included because she was designated by her father as the royal heir. But as you will read, she was not a pharaoh, only a regent for the future heir to the throne.

Timeline of Pharaohs and Moses
in the 18th Dynasty

BC	Moses	Ahmose	Amen I	Thut I	Hat	Thut II	Thut III	Amen II	Thut IV	Amen III	Tut
1539	Moses	1				Moses					
1526	Birth	14	1								
1525	1	15	2								
1524	2	16	3								
1523	3	17	4								
1522	4	18	5								
1521	5	19	6								
1520	6	20	7								
1519	7	21	8								
1518	8	22	9								
1517	9	23	10								
1516	10	24	11								
1515	11	25	12								
1514	12	Died- 26	13	1							
1513	13		14	2							
1512	14		15	3							
1511	15		16	4							
1510	16		17	5							
1509	17		18	6							
1508	18		19	7	1						
1507	19		20	8	2						
1506	20		21	9	3						
1505	21		22	10	4						
1504	22		23	11	5						
1503	23		24	12	6						
1502	24		25	13	7						
1501	25		26	14	8						
1500	26		27	15	9						
1499	27		28	16	10						
1498	28		29	17	11						
1497	29		30	18	12	1					
1496	30		31	19	13	2					
1495	31		32	20	14	3					
1494	32		33	21	15	4					
1493	33		34	22	16	5					
1492	34		35	23	17	6					
1491	35		36	24	18	7					
1490	36		37	25	19	8					
1489	37		38	26	20	9					
1488	38		39	27	21	10					
1487	39		40	28	22	11	22				
1486	40		41	29	23	12	23				

The purple column at left is the age of Moses.

When Moses becomes Thutmose II, that column is also purple.

The first 13 years of Ahmose's reign have been condensed as there are no dates of significance except the birth of Moses in his 1st year of reign and the year he died.

BC	Moses	Ahmose	Amen I	Thut I	Hat	Thut II	Thut III	Amen II	Thut IV	Amen III	Tut
1485	41		42	30			24				
1484	42		43	31			25	1	1		
1483	43						26	2	2		
1482	44						27	3	3		
1481	45						28	4	4		
1480	46						29	5	5		
1479	47						30	6	6		
1478	48						31	7	7		
1477	49						32	8	8		
1476	50						33	9	9		
1475	51						34	10	10		
1474	52						35	11	11		
1473	53						36	12	12		
1472	54						37	13	13		
1471	55						38	14	14		
1470	56						39	15	15		
1469	57						40	16	16		
1468	58						41	17	17		
1467	59						42	18	18		
1466	60						43	19	19		
1465	61						44	20	20		
1464	62						45	21	21		
1463	63						46	22	22		
1462	64						47	23	23		
1461	65						48	24	24		
1460	66						49	25	25		
1459	67						50	26	26		
1458	68						51	27	27		
1457	69						52	28	28		
1456	70						53	29	29		
1455	71						54	30	30	1	1
1454	72								31	2	2
1453	73								32	3	3
1452	74								33	4	4
1451	75								34	5	5
1450	76								35	6	6
1449	77								36	7	7
1448	78								37	8	8
1447	79								38	9	9
1446	80	EXODUS							39	10	10

Mary Nell Lee

Table of Faces of the 18th Dynasty

Two people side by side indicates they
are the same person.

Ahmose- 1st pharaoh of the
18th Dynasty.

1539 - 1514 BC

Amenhotep I/Thutmose I-
Son of Ahmose above.
Daughter rescued Moses.

Amen I- 1526 - 1484 BC
Thut I- 1514 - 1484 BC

**Neferure/Hatshespsut/
Maat-Ka-Re-**
Pharaoh's daughter.
Rescued Moses from the Nile.

Maatkare-1508 - 1486 BC

Senenmut/ Thutmose II-
Moses

Thut II- 1497 - 1486 BC

Thutmose III/Amenhotep II-
Was to be co-regent for Thutmose II.
Became emperor when
Amenhotep 1/ Thutmose I died.

Thut III- 1487 - 1455 BC
Amen II- 1484 - 1455 BC

Thutmose IV/Amenhotep III
Co-regent for Amenhotep II
Emperor pharaoh of the Exodus
Father of Tutankhamun
Father of Akhenaton

Thut IV- 1484 - 1446 BC
Amen III- 1455- 1446 BC

Tutankhamun- co-regent for
his father, Amenhotep III.
Died in the plague of the firstborn.

Tut- 1455- 1446 BC

Ay- brother of Thutmose IV's/
Amenhotep III's wife, Tiye/Tiaa/Tey
Uncle of Tutankhamun.
Uncle of next pharaoh, Akhenaton.

Date of reign not clear

Akhenaton- son of Thutmose IV/
Amenhotep III.
Brother of Tutankhamun.

Date of reign not clear

Horemheb- Many positions in
Tutankhamun's reign, general of the
army in Tut's, Ay's and Akhenaton's
reign.
Appointed Paramesse as his successor
and he became 1st pharaoh of the
19th dynasty, Ramesses I.

Date of reign not clear

*Attribution of all photos on pages 60 and 61 is
noted on the larger version of the photos elsewhere
in the book.*

Chapter 7

ISRAEL ENSLAVED

*Metropolitan
Museum of Art*

Ahmose I
Nebpehtyre

When Ahmose completed the expulsion of the Hyksos and regained control of northern Egypt, he let the children of Israel who lived alongside the Hyksos to remain in the country because it had been decreed by Pharaoh Djoser. In fact, scholars question the expulsion of the Hyksos because of evidence that an Asian presence continued to live there. This verifies the presence of Hebrews, the Israelites, still being in the region.

When he came to the throne, Ahmose had no co-regent as the northern region was under the control of the Hyksos. But when he expelled the Hyksos, he needed to appoint a co-regent to rule in the north. Beginning with that co-regent, kings would have two names for two positions as pharaoh.

Ahmose then enslaved the Israelites. They were meek, peaceful and non-rebellious but he was afraid of them. He believed they were capable of conquering the Egyptian nation because they were strong and their numbers grew rapidly. Hence he also ordered the deaths of all newborn males:

Exodus 1:7 And the children of Israel were fruitful, and increased abundantly, and multiplied, and waxed exceeding mighty; and the land was filled with them. 8 Now there arose up a new king over Egypt, which knew not Joseph. 9 And he said unto his people, Behold, the people of the children of Israel are more and mightier than we: 10 Come on, let us deal wisely with them; lest they multiply, and it come to pass, that, when there falleth out any war, they join also unto our enemies, and fight against us, and so get them up out of the land. 11 Therefore they did set over them taskmasters to afflict them with their burdens. And they built for Pharaoh treasure cities, Pithom and Raamses. 12 But the more they afflicted them, the more they multiplied and grew. And they were grieved because of the children of Israel. 13 And the Egyptians made the children of Israel to serve with rigour: 14 And they made their lives bitter with hard bondage, in morter, and in brick, and in all manner of service in the field: all their service, wherein they made them serve, was with rigour. 15 And the king of Egypt spake to the Hebrew midwives, of which the name of the one was Shiphrah, and the name of the other Puah: 16 And he said, When ye do the office of a midwife to the Hebrew women, and see them upon the stools; if it be a son, then ye shall kill him: but if it be a daughter, then she shall live. 17 But the midwives feared God, and did not as the king of Egypt commanded them, but saved the men children alive. 18 And the king of Egypt called for the midwives, and said unto them, Why have ye done this thing, and have saved the men children alive? 19 And the midwives said unto Pharaoh, Because the Hebrew women are not as the Egyptian women; for they are lively, and are delivered ere the midwives come in unto them. 20 Therefore God dealt well with the midwives: and the people multiplied, and waxed very mighty. 21 And it came to pass, because the midwives feared God, that he made them houses. 22 And Pharaoh charged all his people, saying, Every son that is born ye shall cast into the river, and every daughter ye shall save alive.

Amenhotep I,
Son of Ahmose, became Co-Regent

With the northern territory reconquered and the country unified, it became necessary for the Theban pharaoh Ahmose to appoint a co-regent to manage the affairs of the north. We know that Ahmose continued his military exploits which made it especially needful to have a co-regent.

Randall Lee

Amenhotep I
Djeserkare

In addition, in the event something happened to the emperor pharaoh, it was imperative that there was someone capable of stepping in who had the proper credentials.

He appointed his son to this position and he took the name Amenhotep I. This son became the pharaoh in Memphis and he was co-regent to the senior Pharaoh Ahmose who ruled in Thebes. The distance between Memphis where Amenhotep lived and Thebes where Ahmose lived was about 375 miles, a great distance in historic times.

The Birth of Moses in 1526 BC

It was Amenhotep I who had to enforce Ahmose's orders to the midwives to kill the newborn Hebrew males because he lived in the north where the Israelites were located.

Based on the date of the Exodus, 1526 BC was the year Ahmose issued his edict that all the Hebrew male babies were to be killed and it was also the year Moses was born. This was eighty years from the date of the future Exodus.

Pharaoh's daughter rescued Moses soon after she and her family moved to the palace in Memphis when her father became the northern pharaoh. It could not have been the Theban pharaoh whose daughter rescued Moses because the Israelites lived in the northern Delta area.

Exodus chapter 2 tells of the birth of Moses and how his mother made an ark of bulrushes and placed him in the Nile River where pharaoh's daughter saw him and rescued him. His sister, knowing he still needed to be nursed, asked the pharaoh's daughter if she would like her to find a nurse of the Hebrew women to take care of the baby for her.

This resulted in her bringing Moses' real mother. Pharaoh's daughter then told her to take the child and nurse it and she would pay her wages to do so. Because of the command by Ahmose to kill all of the male newborns, it is likely that the co-regent pharaoh's daughter knew she could not bring the child into the northern palace at that time. In fact, Moses would continue to live with his real mother a number of years.

From this time onward, the pharaohs of the 18th Dynasty ruled first in Memphis as co-regent and then moved to Thebes when they became the emperor pharaoh. One name was given to the co-regent and when he then became emperor pharaoh, he was given another name.

A reminder- what this means is that the same person had both a Thutmose and an Amenhotep name depending on their position as pharaoh. Another important thing to remember is that all events were dated according to the year of the pharaoh's reign. To further complicate matters, once the pharaoh became the emperor in Thebes, he had two distinct timelines of regnal years-one chronology of years in one name which began when he became co-regent and another chronology of regnal years when he became emperor in Thebes. This is a vital point to keep in mind.

The records for Amenhotep I don't reveal any military actions on his part in Canaan or Syria. However, in the tombs of two of his officials are inscriptions stating he led excursions into Nubia and Kehek, but the identification of Kehek is not known. In his year 7, he subdued Nubia and secured it completely under Egyptian control. This is not a lot of documentation but the emphasis was on the regnal years of his father as the emperor.

During his reign as Amenhotep I, his father, Ahmose was still alive and carrying on the major military actions needed to firm up Egypt's control of Canaan and Syria where the Hyksos had fled.

Amenhotep I became Emperor Thutmose I

Amenhotep I lived in Memphis until Ahmose died. Once the senior pharaoh in Thebes had died, Amenhotep I took the additional name Thutmose I and moved to Thebes as the emperor. I do not know how their names were decided or who chose them, only that they reflect the name of the gods their family revered.

The year he was crowned as the senior pharaoh, Nubia rebelled. I presume they thought the country was weak with the death of Ahmose. But Thutmose I sailed up the Nile to Nubia and brought the rebellion under control. He personally killed the Nubian king and displayed his body hanging it head down on the prow of his ship when he returned to Thebes. To help facilitate ease in traveling to Nubia, he dredged the canal at the First Cataract that Sesostris III built.

In his year 2, his second campaign was north where he crossed the Euphrates River into Naharin, Mitanni territory and the Syrian princes all gave their allegiance to him although they later withdrew it. He celebrated his victory on the way back to Egypt. He stopped in Niy in Syria for an elephant hunt. He was obviously a military leader of substantial genius.

The 18th Dynasty was now on its way to becoming a very great nation. A major factor was their slave force, the Israelites.

Amenhotep 1
Became Emperor Thutmose I

Mary Nell Lee

Tuthmosis I
Akheperkare

Moses Moved to the Palace

When he became emperor, Pharaoh Thutmose I, and moved to Thebes, Moses was twelve years old and it was at this time that he came to the palace to live. It makes sense that he did not come at an earlier age when we consider the Biblical account of the faith of Moses and his love for the God of Abraham. The only time he would have had to learn about the God of his fathers was when he was at home with his mother.

Another point to consider is that co-regent Amenhotep I would not have allowed the child into the palace while his father and senior pharaoh Ahmose was alive. After all, Ahmose had enslaved the Hebrews and ordered the death of all Hebrew males babies at birth. Even though Ahmose was living 375 miles south of the northern palace, word would surely have filtered back to him. Only when Amenhotep I became the Theban emperor, with the additional title of Thutmose I, was he free to bring Moses into the palace.

When we read historical data, the emotions and feelings of the people we are reading about seem nonexistent. As I compiled this research, a beautiful story emerged of a young girl who fell in love with a beautiful baby who was floating in the Nile River, knowing full well that it was a Hebrew child.

She understood that the mother was resorting to such a dangerous option to try to save her baby from certain death. Not only did I sense the great love this girl had for baby Moses, I came to the conclusion that her father, Thutmose I, was very tender when it came to his daughter because he also knew the child was a Hebrew and yet he allowed her to adopt him. One thing I learned from Ron was that we must never forget that these ancient people were still "just people" like us with the same feelings and emotions.

The most incredible thing I gained from all the research into this subject was an appreciation of the ancient personalities and the insights into their lives and their characters.

A Timeline Confirmation

After I had constructed my first proposed timeline, I began to refine it. In the early years of my research, I found a very crucial piece of information confirming the dating of the reign of Amenhotep I which provided another anchor point in my chronology. In the "Encyclopaedia Britannica" 1985 ed. vol. 4 pp. 575- 6:

"The next date is given by a medical papyrus, to which a calendar is added, possibly to insure a correct conversion of dates used in the receipts to the actual timetable. Here it is said that the 9th day of the 11th month of year 9 of King Amenhotep I was the day of the helical rising of Sothis- i.e., 1538 BC. This date, however, is only accurate provided the astronomical observations were taken at the old residence of Memphis; if observed at Thebes in Upper Egypt, the residence of the 18th dynasty, the date must be lowered by 20 years- i.e., 1518 BC."

My timeline already showed the 9th year of Amenhotep I was 1518 BC, the exact date recorded in the papyrus if the observance of the day of the heliacal rising was noted at Thebes. This was an amazing confirmation for me and a great encouragement since I found a number of issues in the ancient records that caused problems because the data was lacking.

Confusion over to Whom Regnal Years Apply

In addition to the lack of documentation, as in the case of Amenhotep I's reign, I propose that some of the regnal years of some pharaohs are assigned to the wrong pharaoh. I concluded this because in some of the monuments and records the pharaoh's name is not mentioned, only the regnal date. Since I am proposing the pharaoh has two names with two different lists of regnal years, sometimes a pharaoh's regnal year is attributed to him in his other capacity. Sometimes it is attributed to an entirely different king.

Yet another cause of confusion comes from the tombs of some officials. In their tombs, they listed their accomplishments on the wall for the gods to know their great works. In some of these inscriptions these officials list their exploits under each pharaoh as if each Thutmose and Amenhotep are separate individuals when in fact it is relating events under each king in each of his two positions. Because scholars and archaeologists rely so much on these tomb inscriptions, it is difficult to overcome the bias even for me as I did my research. But the bulk of the data gleaned from monuments and temple walls was straight forward as I studied.

I again want to stress that the reader needs to keep in mind that Ron's theory has most pharaohs having different names as co-regent and then as emperor pharaoh.

Recap of Who's Who in Chapter 7

Left- Ahmose- the 1st king of the 18th dynasty. He expelled the Hyksos from Egypt and enslaved the Israelites.

Below left- Ahmose's son, Amenhotep I whom he appointed to be his co-regent in the north (Memphis).

Below- Thutmose I, the same person as Amenhotep I. He took the additional name when he became the "emperor" or the main pharaoh.

Amenhotep I and Thutmose I are the same person. He later seemed to prefer his name of Thutmose I which was his name as Emperor. More of his reign is recorded in this name than in his name of Amenhotep I.

Mary Nell Lee
An ark-like basket in the Cairo Museum from the 18th Dynasty. This is the size that could have easily held a baby. It is an example of what the ark that held baby Moses may have looked like.

Chapter 8

PHARAOH'S DAUGHTER

Metropolitan
Museum of Art

Queen
Hatshepsut
Maatkare

Neferure = Hatshepsut = Maatkare

Hatshepsut was the name she used the most in her monuments and inscriptions. She has been written up to be a ruthless, ambitious woman who wanted to secure the throne for herself. It is also believed that Neferure was her daughter although there is no record of her having a child. It is very complicated to untangle the different theories concerning Hatshepsut but as the story unfolds, I propose that the evidences tell a different story.

A great deal of what we know about Hatshepsut comes from her mortuary temple, Djeser-Djeseru, located beneath the cliffs of Deir el-Bahri across the Nile from Thebes.

Neferure Rescued Moses

Pharaoh's daughter, first called Nefurure in Memphis, had not been able to bring her adopted son, Moses, into the royal palace during the time Ahmose was alive. But with her father now the emperor, young Neferure removed Moses from his home in the Delta region to the palace in Thebes. There she proceeded to raise him as her own.

Since he was about 12 years old at that time, it must have been traumatic for Moses and his family, but there is evidence that he did not lose touch with his family. We have very little information on his first few years in the palace but when he was about eighteen, something very unusual happened.

Thutmose I Had No Royal Heir

As emperor or senior pharaoh, Thutmose I had no male heir to rule in Memphis so none was appointed. The ancient records in the name Thutmose I, which are more plenteous than those in his Amenhotep I name, suggested he had sons but they died young.

This presented a problem because the royal line was passed through the royal mother who was the daughter of the pharaoh and the great royal wife. The only way this was possible was through brother/sister marriages. Perhaps genetic problems arose with inbreeding that caused this lack of sons or sons who died early. But I suggest that God brought about the events which would serve to bring Moses into the royal family and prepare him for the job that lay head.

Wikimedia Commons- Marc Ryckaert / CC BY-SA

Hatshepsut's Mortuary Temple, Djeser-Djeseru across the Nile from ancient Thebes.

Wikimedia Commons- Fanny Schertzer / CC BY-SA

The front of Hatshepsut's mortuary temple, lined with statues depicting Osiris. He represented the Egyptian king after death.

Hatshepsut Declared Royal Heir

In year 7 of Thutmose I, the pharaoh declared his daughter to be the heir to the throne. The Theban pharaoh was unable to appoint a pharaoh in Memphis because of the lack of a male heir. Instead, he secured the north with strong and faithful officials he had come to know and trust when he was ruling in the northern city.

But he had to prepare for the security of Egypt's future by preparing the way for a future pharaoh. His daughter, Neferure, was given the name Hatshepsut when they moved to Thebes even though her name, Neferure, continued to appear. She was given the additional royal name of Maatkare when she became the royal heir in regnal year 7 of Thutmose I.

The story of Hatshepsut and how she became "king" is taken from a wall in her mortuary temple at Deir el Bahri, Djeser Djeseru depicting her direct descent from the gods. Her birth is presented in figures on the wall and the scene begins with a gathering of various gods in the presence of Amun, the supreme god of Thebes. As the scenes progress, the god Thoth leads Amun into the chamber of Hatshepsut's mother, Queen Ahmose.

Randall Lee

Hathsehepsut's mother, Queen Ahmose is visibly pregnant and is being led by the gods and goddesses to give birth to the royal child.

Queen Ahmose is here shown sitting on the birthing stool. The gods and goddesses and all in attendence will care for her through the birthing process.

The next scene depicts Amun seated facing the queen and impregnating her with the "ankh" by holding it to her nose. The ankh is the symbol of the divine breath of life.

The god Khnum then fashions Hatshepsut and her Ka on the pottery wheel. Then the goddess Heqt puts the breath of life in the baby.

The following scene has Toth appearing to the pregnant queen informing her the time for the birth was at hand. Khnum and Heqt then lead her to the birth chamber.

At the end, the baby is presented and although the name of the baby is Hatshepsut, **the baby portrayed is a male.** In another scene, it is Hatshepsut holding the baby! These points are evidence of a great misinterpretation and misunderstanding and there is only one scenario that can be factual.

Two babies are depicted which represent the 'ba' and the 'ka' of the child. Ancient Egyptians believed these were parts of the soul of a person.

The ka was supposedly the life force of the person. It survived death but was confined to the tomb until after the judgment. The burial preparations were made to provide for the ka to be able to have a home, so to speak. A mummy was needed but evidence showed that it could be supplied by the body of another if needed.

The ba could travel freely, leave the tomb and visit wherever it wanted to go. It could even visit the underworld if it wanted to. It supposedly kept returning to the tomb, time and time again, until it was reunited with the ka.

Their judgment scenes depict the "weighing of the heart" to determine the fate of the deceased. Tombs are full of inscriptions of occupants telling of their good deeds throughout to hopefully influence the outcome of their judgment. After this judgment, the ka and ba can reunite and enter the happy afterworld as long as all goes well.

The most important aspect of the birth scenes depicting Hatshepsut is the fact that she is presented as a male child. It is not acceptable to suppose that the artists made a mistake. This fact alone is evidence of something else. I propose that it was because, in time, another name would be chiseled into the wall, replacing Hatshepsut's name. I believe the name of the future monarch was intended to be placed upon the walls one day- that future monarch being her adopted son, Moses, who was being groomed to take the throne upon the death of her father.

Public Domain

The wall painting depicting the presentation of the baby Hatshepsut to the parents. As is evident, the baby(s) presented is a boy.

Hatshepsut's Father
on the Walls of Her Temple

Misconceptions concerning Hatshepsut began when her mortuary temple was first rediscovered in recent history. One major issue deals with the identity of a king appearing on the walls of her temple that I believe refers to her father, Thutmose I. Although he had the additional name of Amenhotep I, as emperor pharaoh he favored his Thutmose name for most of his monuments.

Some archaeologists and scholars noted that in some instances the name referring to "Thutmose I" is written differently to the way they are used to. For this reason, they claim it is not her father being depicted but instead a future king by the name of Thutmose III.

The spelling "Menkheperkare" has an additional "ka" within the name that differs from her father's usual spelling. Amazingly, scholars have accepted as fact that it is not referring to her father but is actually a variation on the name Thutmose III, "Menkheperre." I strongly disagree.

This is a crucial issue. I propose these inscriptions in her mortuary temple are actually referring to Hatshepsut's father, Thutmose I and are a variation of his name. This matter changes a large part of the picture of Hatshepsut's life. Amenhotep I was the first king to take the Thutmose name upon becoming emperor and I propose that the name evolved, taking slightly different forms during his reign and depending on the scribes.

It was her father in all the inscriptions of her early life in her temple. Thutmose III is included on her temple walls many years later when he comes to the throne but that is many years later.

A relief on the wall of Hatshepsut's temple, seen at right, shows Queen Ahmose and Thutmose I, her parents, and a little girl bearing the name Neferubity. I propose that this is young Neferure with a different spelling of her name. I see no reason why another child would be pictured in her temple, especially one not mentioned elsewhere.

K. R. Lepsius- Public Domain

Also, it must be understood that this temple is full of erasures and changes of different royal names in various places. Scholars have interpreted this as an attack on Hatshepsut's memory but I believe it is the result of a totally different issue which will become clear later.

There are many statues still in existence that are said to be Hatshepsut. They have her cartouche on them. However, I do not believe they represent what Hatshepsut looked like at all. I believe another person was the model.

The story in every ancient Egyptian history book tells of Hatshepsut, the woman who wanted to be king, who wanted to rule the country. She is portrayed as overambitious, ruthless and making many enemies along the way.

But I believe the evidence, the same evidence used to draw this conclusion, tells a different story. I believe she was a sweet young girl who fell in love with a beautiful Hebrew baby.

Recap of Who's Who in Chapter 8

Hatshepsut- granddaughter of Ahmose and the daughter of Amenhotep I, who is also Thutmose I.
- She was the "pharaoh's daughter" who rescued the Hebrew baby, Moses, from the Nile.
- She was also named Neferure when she was young. In later years, she was given a royal name, Maatkare.
- In the photo on the next page, she is depicted holding young Moses.

Wikimedia Commons- Postdlf / CC BY-SA

Chapter 9

SENENMUT IS MOSES

Pharaoh's Daughter (Neferure) Holding
Baby Moses (Senenmut)

Connected to Hatshepsut and her mortuary temple is one of the most amazing people ever found in the ancient Egyptian records who was not a pharaoh, named Senenmut. I spent many years in great excitement and anticipation of learning more about this man. I soon became completely satisfied that Senenmut was Moses so every morsel of information I gleaned was like a gift.

Our first glimpses of Senenmut come from a large number of statues with the names of Senenmut and Neferure. These statues are the first of their kind in ancient Egypt and depict a person holding a child with the royal sidelock of youth. I propose that these depict young Hatshepsut, referred to as Neferure, holding her adopted son, Moses. These statues are stated by scholars as being Senenmut holding a young Neferure

Wikimedia Commons– Daniel Mayer / CC BY-SA

Neferure holding baby Senenmut. Outside of the Cairo Museum.

and the claim is that he is her nurse or tutor. I believe the inscriptions on them have been misinterpreted.

To understand if the inscriptions could possibly be incorrectly translated I researched hieroglyphs but it was beyond my understanding. I needed to speak with someone educated in the ancient Egyptian writing but I knew I had to be careful who I spoke with. If they knew why I was making inquiries, I knew I could not get the honest responses I was looking for.

Then I had a miraculous opportunity arise. While in one of the Harvard Museums, I struck up a conversation with a Harvard PhD student who was translating a stele in the museum. It was a stele that had been translated long ago which gave me a reason to ask a question. I asked why she was translating something that had already been translated. This started a very fruitful exchange. I asked her if it was possible to accurately translate ancient hieroglyphics and be confident that the translation was accurate.

She answered "No, not really." The PhD student explained to me that while we think we know what different symbols mean, we cannot truly understand their structure. Also it depends on the translator. One sign can either mean a word or a sound and it is up to the translator to decide which it is. Add to this, the fact that different scribes had different writing methods.

Left- Neferure and baby Senenmut at the British Museum.

Wikimedia Commons- British Museum / CC BY-SA

Wikimedia Commons- Ovedc/ CC BY-SA

Above- Neferure and baby Senenmut in the Cairo Museum.
Left- Neferure and baby Senenmut in the Pergamon Museum, Berlin.

Wikimedia Commons- Andreas Praefcke/ Public Domain

It was this situation with the statues of Neferure and Senenmut that I was referring to when I spoke with this PhD student. Without mentioning the specifics, I asked if it was possible that the inscriptions on a statue could be read incorrectly, applying the identifications erroneously? Her answer was, "Yes, it is possible."

These statues clearly represent a woman holding a child that she loves very much. Since this type of statue appears for the first time at this particular point in Egyptian history and since they all appear to portray a woman with a child, I think there is no doubt that these statues represent young Neferure holding her much loved adopted son, Senenmut (Moses).

Hatshepsut Declared the Royal Heir

Not much is known about Senenmut during his earliest years in the palace with his adopted mother. In the 7th year his adopted grandfather reigned as emperor pharaoh under the name of Thutmose I and events take place that indicate important plans for the future of the throne of Egypt. A plan was devised by which to prepare for a future monarch.

Thutmose I had no co-regent nor male heir. He needed an heir as he had to prepare for the future of the now unified Egypt. A woman was not a viable option as a future king, however, the royal line traditionally flowed through the royal daughter. I propose that this is the reason he elevated his daughter formally on the walls of her temple.

Scholars state Hatshepsut declared herself to be king. However, I propose that this was done by her father. She was given an additional name, Maatkare, for this new position as the heir to the throne. I don't believe she was ever intended to rule as the king, only as a regent for a male candidate.

It is true that she is depicted on the walls and monuments as a man. This is puzzling when taken at face value and this is what I believe caused such mass confusion among the explanations of what it meant. But when it is looked at differently, it becomes apparent that there is a chronology to these events that I believe has not been understood.

I propose the following for the chain of events:

- Neferure was a young girl who rescued Moses.
- Hatshepsut was the royal name given the daughter of the emperor when they moved to Thebes with her young adopted son.

BC	Moses	Ahmose	Amen I	Thut I	Hat
1539		1			
1526	Birth	14	1		
1525	1	15	2		
1524	2	16	3		
1523	3	17	4		
1522	4	18	5		
1521	5	19	6		
1520	6	20	7		
1519	7	21	8		
1518	8	22	9		
1517	9	23	10		
1516	10	24	11		
1515	11	25	12		
1514	12	Died- 26	13	1	
1513	13		14	2	
1512	14		15	3	
1511	15		16	4	
1510	16		17	5	
1509	17		18	6	
1508	18		19	7	1

Mary Nell Lee

In this timeline segment, it can be seen that year 7 of Thutmose I was the year that Hatshepsut began her regnal years as the royal heir.

At this time Moses was 18 years old and had been living in the palace for 6 years, since he was 12 years old.

Year 7 of Thutmose I was also year 19 of his reign as Amenhotep I.

- Her adopted son's great abilities and integrity made him the pharaoh's great hope for the future throne.
- To begin preparations for this possibility, Hatshepsut was promoted to be the heir, Maatkare, who had the right of rulership passed through her.
- She would act as regent for the heir apparent, Senenmut, her adopted son, Moses.
- When he came to the throne, my proposition is all the statues and representations of Hatshepsut as a man would have the name changed to Moses' royal name.

Year 7 of Thutmose I's reign as emperor was considered year 1 of the reign of Hatshepsut as heir to the throne. This was a new concept and there wasn't a prescribed way of handling it. My theory is that the names and pictures on the wall of her temple applying to her as a king would have been adjusted when the future pharaoh was came to the throne. This will be shown later to have occurred in numerous places. It is worth noting that she is not listed in either the Saqqara Tablet list of kings or the Abydos kings list and thus was never recognized as a ruler.

If Moses was going to ascend to the throne as the future king, the pharaoh would want to be sure this young Hebrew man was capable of rulership. He would also need to be sure he would give his full allegiance to the Egyptian throne before elevating him to such a position.

Senenmut's abilities and intelligence were clearly well above average and he was accepted by his adopted grandfather as the obvious choice. Arranging for the future monarch to go through his daughter, I believe, was a brilliant plan.

But as this was only Thutmose I's regnal year 7 and Moses was only 18 years old, the evidence shows that the Egyptian king patiently watched his young adopted grandson, Senenmut, grow and thrive.

As time progressed, statues and inscriptions appeared listing the many accomplishments of Senenmut. He had at least 90 different titles:

"Hereditary prince, chief steward who conducted all the works of the king, one who heard the hearing alone in the privy council, chief of the whole land, steward of Amun, wearer of the royal seal, overseer of the works of Amun, overseer of the granary of Amun, overseer of the storehouse of Amun, overseer of all [works] of the house of silver, overseer of the gardens of Amun, Overseer of the cattle of Amun, Chief of the peasant-serfs of Amun, overseer of the temples of Neit, chief steward of the Princess, Nefrure, chief steward who conducted all the works of the king, real confidant of the king, privy councilor of the right hand", and more.

TT71 Tomb Begun for Senenmut

Also in this same regnal year 7, a tomb was begun for Senenmut. Already the inscriptions in the tomb reveal that Senenmut was a most remarkable person. Its location indicates he was very close to the royal family. The first inscription in the tomb reads:

[...] who are in the sacre[dland...Senenmu]t[...] for the steward [of Amuns Senenmut, justified,] engendered [of the] dignitary [Ramose.. .] his [...] of darkness,! that he might see the sun's disk, that he might adore Ra, that he might propitiate the one who has risen from Nun, that he might make his appearances according as he desires, that he might exercise his will" in his tomb, that [his] ka might be content" [. . .] the overseer of the granaries of [Amun Senenmut]. (The Tombs of Senenmut, Peter Dorman, p, 31.)

Elin Tourniaire Haugvik Berglund

The first tomb constructed for Senenmut in Sheikh Abd el-Qurna across the Nile from Thebes.

In text six, it says: *Hereditary prince cou[nt] . . . steward . . . Hereditary prince, count. . .] stew[ard . . .] Senen[mut . ....]*

The word "hereditary" is the first indication that Senenmut is being prepared for something pertaining to the royal family. The next text, number 7, makes it clear that he is already determined to wield power as the palace is mentioned:

Hereditary prince, count who has authority in the palace, overseer of the granaries of [Amun], Sen[enmut], justified; his [mother],*

Elin Tourniaire Haugvik Berglund

Wind eroded statue of Hatshepsut holding Senenmut as a baby, which is at the above tomb.

mistress of the house Hatnofer. [Making] a htp-dj-nsw offering, doubly pure [. '(...) (. . .) [. . .]Minhote[p . . .] [Columns 11-13 are destroyed.] 1[. . . the stew]ard [Senenmut, justified;] his beloved father, Ramose, justified.

It is important to note the mention of his parents, Hatnofer and Ramose. Thutmose I and his daughter Hatshepsut honored Moses' desire to be known as the son of his own parents which I find remarkable. Also mentioned in different texts are his brother, called Amenemhat and 'his beloved sister, Ahhotep." We know from the Biblical account Moses had a brother, Aaron, and a sister, Miriam. This paints a picture of a loving adopted mother and adopted grandfather by allowing the portrayal of his real family in his tomb.

I propose that this has great significance to the story of Moses.

HEB 11:24 By faith Moses, when he was come to years, refused to be called the son of Pharaoh's daughter;

I believe the name he was given, Senenmut, is highly significant. The Egyptian name of Senenmut means "mother's brother." The Scripture states that Moses refused to be known as the son of pharaoh's daughter, Hatshepsut. Instead he insisted on keeping his connection to his own parents and nationality. He was a Hebrew and worshiped the God of Abraham and that would forever be his identity.

I do believe he loved Hatshepsut very much and was deeply grateful to her for saving his life. I also believe her love for Moses was an unselfish love. By the name he was given, I believe his relationship with pharaoh's daughter was related in a manner which was acceptable to him.

The Tomb of Hatnofer and Ramose
Senenmut's Parents (Jochebed and Amram)

A discovery which certainly indicates Hatshepsut's love for her adopted son was made in January 1936 by Ambrose Lansing and William Hayes while excavating across the Nile from ancient Thebes for the Metropolitan Museum of Art. They found a tomb which contained two beautiful sarcophaguses and two uninscribed plain white coffins. The inscriptions in this simple tomb show that it was made in year 7 of an unnamed pharaoh (Thutmose I) for a lady named Hatnofer.

This was the same year Senenmut's tomb was begun. When I learned of this discovery, I was again extremely excited to learn all I could about it. I truly believed these were the people mentioned by name in the Bible as the parents of Moses.

It was very difficult to find information about the tomb and its discovery. Finally I found the original report with photographs. I was in awe as I read the report and studied the photos. The evidence shed a great deal of light on Moses' family.

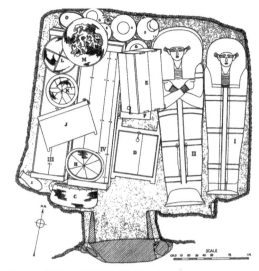

Lansing & Hayes 1937, Public Domain

Diagram of the tomb when first found.

Hatnofer was the mother of Senenmut which means she was the mother of Moses who was now eighteen years old in year 7 of Thutmose I.

Lansing & Hayes 1937, Public Domain

The covered coffins of Hatnofer and Ramose when they were found.

Funeral provisions setting on the coffins in Hatnofer and Ramose's tomb.

Her mummy was preserved in a wonderful manner and it could be seen that she was treated with extreme care. Her coffin was a beautiful painted sarcophagus and inside her mummy wore a beautiful gold leafed mummy mask. The tomb was full of all the items normally included in a royal or near royal burial.

However, the burial did not contain the wall paintings normally associated with a royal burial. It was a small chamber just large enough to contain everything within it.

In another beautiful painted coffin was the mummy of Ramose, Moses' father. However, his mummy was not in the same condition as Hatnofer's. In fact his was just mainly bones:

"By contrast, although given the same elaborate exterior wrappings, Ramose's

mummy was discovered to be largely skeletonized, with a great loss of skin and flesh from the bones; his most distinguishing feature was a thick thatch of brown hair. Nor was the body completely intact at the time of wrapping, since some bones were actually misplaced among the numerous linen layers. Unlike Hatnofer, the father's mummy was not adorned with jewelry, a funeral mask, papyrus roll, or inscribed shroud..." ("Family burial and Commemoration in the Theban Necropolis" by Peter Dorman, on page 6.)

It is evident from Ramose's remains that he was exhumed from an original grave and brought to this tomb at the time of Hatnofer's burial. The other two coffins contained the remains of three young women and three children:

"Even more cursory was the wrapping of the six anonymous mummies in the chamber, which proved to be those of three young women and three children. Their remains consisted of little more than piles of bones, with little flesh or connective tissue to hold them together, apparently gathered together and bundled up in linen in a compressed state. Among the disjointed mummies the excavators found masses of straw, reed matting, dirt, sand and gravel, and at least one mummy had been braced with palm reeds. These jumbled collections of bones are clearly not reflective of normal embalming practice, but rather indicate exhumation from some other location, perhaps with the remnants of their original reed matting included among their dislocated bones." (Dorman, p. 6.)

It can be surmised that Ramose died before his wife, Hatnofer. This may have been prior to Moses' rise in esteem with the pharaoh. His body was clearly not embalmed and

Lansing & Hayes 1937, Public Domain

The mummy of Hatnofer with her gold mask.

mummified which could mean, being a Hebrew, he was simply buried in the ground.

The same can be said about the bodies in the white coffins, that they all were exhumed from burials in the earth, and brought here upon Hatnofer's death.

The fact that Hatnofer was mummified and so well preserved indicates that she likely was living near Moses in Thebes when she died. Her husband had died prior to this time and was buried in the Delta area near his home. The other unidentified mummies were likely also buried in the northern home of the Israelites.

The burial shows that Senenmut's family was highly revered by the royal family at the time of this burial even though they had no royal titles. Hatnofer (Jochebed) was titled "housemistress" while Ramose (Amram) was referred to as "the worthy."

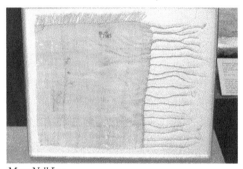
Mary Nell Lee

Mary Nell Lee

Above and below are various items from Hatnofer and Ramose's tomb.

Mary Nell Lee

Mary Nell Lee

Above is the mummy mask that was on Hatnofer.

All the items from this tomb are on display at the Metropolitan Museum of Art in New York City. The excavation when they were found was sponsored by the MET.

The names found on articles within the tomb included Neferure, Hatshepsut and Maatkare, the royal name Hatshepsut acquired that same year. This indicates that items were chosen from the royal treasury from before and after her name change to Maatkare which occurred around this time.

The identification of this as Senenmut's family was made when the excavators remembered a panel in another tomb they had uncovered about 10 years earlier. In this tomb, Senemut's Deir el-Bahri tomb (TT353), there was a panel depicting the parents of Senenmut, Hatnofer and Ramose, with their son.

This tomb is located directly below the tomb constructed for Senenmut, known as Theban Tomb 71 (TT71), the first tomb constructed for him. It is located on the west side of the Nile, opposite ancient Thebes, at Sheikh Abd el Qurna. The tomb of Hatnofer and Ramose was covered by chips from Senenmut's tomb, which shows that their tomb was constructed first.

There is a wealth of information gleaned from this burial. Nearby there are even the burials of a horse and a small ape which may have been Senenmut's pets. The coffin of a person named Harmose, who was a singer, was also found in the rubble below Senenmut's tomb.

Inscriptions on Senenmut Statues

An inscription on a statue of Senenmut in the Berlin Museum has this inscription that confirmed one very important feature of my timeline concerning when Moses came to live in the palace:

*"He [the king] has made me the headman of the supervisors and the overseer of works. **I was in this land under his orders since the happening of the death of the one who was before him** and I am living under the Lady of the Two Lands, king of Upper and Lower Egypt (Ma'at-ka-Ra), may she live!"*

My chronological arrangement shows Moses coming into the palace only when Ahmose had died in 1514 BC- *"since the happening of the death of the one who was before him…",* and was then living under the care or regency of his adoptive mother, Maatkare. There is another part of that inscription which is important to note:

"Senmut, triumphant, not found among the writings] of the ancestors,…"

The young Hebrew man was nowhere recorded in the records of the royal families but one day he would be known throughout the entire world.

Josephus wrote that Moses was very popular with the Egyptians and was the general who pacified Nubia, which increased the wealth

Mary Nell Lee
The coffins of Ramose and Hatnofer in the Metropolitan Museum of Art.

of Egypt greatly by the gold paid as tribute by the Nubians. In Djeser-Djeseru the wall with the Punt Reliefs are dated to year 9 (of Thutmose I), and Moses would have been 20 years old. The expedition was most likely undertaken to restore trading associations that had deteriorated and Senenmut's name is mentioned in connection with that expedition.

It gives detailed accounting of all the wonderful things brought back, including large amounts of gold and other precious items. The inscription credits Maatkare (Hatshepsut) with the expedition, although it is likely that she did not actually go. In one final scene, Hatshepsut is sitting on a throne with 3 men standing in front of her. Over the first man is recorded:

Behold, it was commanded, as follows: "They shall give the court L. P. H., to the hereditary prince, count, wearer of the royal seal, sole companion, chief treasurer, Nehsi to dispatch the army [to] Punt."

Over the man in the middle it reads: *"Steward of Amun, Senenmut".* Senenmut, 20 years old at this time, was rising up through the ranks and this was the military expedition that Manetho wrote about.

Another exciting evidence came from the inscription on the statue of Senenmut at the Chicago Field Museum that has been translated to read:

"I was a dignitary beloved of his master, who had access to the miracle of the Lady of the Two Lands. He has made me great, and he has promoted me in the Two Lands. He appointed me to be the overseer of his House to judge the Two Lands in their entirety because of my excellence upon his heart. I have educated the king's eldest daughter, God's Wife [Neferu-Ra], may she live! I was given to her to be the father of the goddesses because of my efficacy for the king." (A Unique Statue of Senmut, by T. G. Allen, in "The American Journal of Semitic Languages and Literatures" 44 (1927), p. 53.)

This above inscription as translated makes no sense. I propose this is another case like the one I discussed earlier about the reversal of the identities of Neferure and Senenmut on the statues of a person holding a young child. I propose that two corrections are warranted. I firmly believe Senenmut is saying he was **"educated BY the king's eldest daughter"** and was **"given to her BY the father of the goddess."**

Hatshepsut needed her father's permission to adopt Moses, hence he was "given to her BY the father of the goddess." Since his adoptive mother would arrange for his education with the finest Egyptian teachers available in all aspects of knowledge a future king would need, the correction: "he was" educated BY the king's eldest daughter" now makes sense.

An Unexpected Discovery

One of the most exciting discoveries (for me) happened one summer in the 1990's. Ron and I had the very great honor of spending time with Dr. Ali Hassan of the Egyptian Antiquities Organization. One day a few months earlier Ron went to meet him for the first time. He was quite surprised at the reception he received. Dr. Hassan stood up and welcomed him quite warmly. He explained to Ron that he was so happy to meet an American at that exact time because his son in the United States needed help.

I was not in Egypt on that trip and Ron called me to help. The result was that his son came to stay with me for a while. A wonderful young nineteen year old, it was an honor to spend time with him and help him with his situation. As a result, his father asked what he could do for me. I asked him to take us to certain places, like Djeser Djeseru and Senemut's second tomb, among other things.

Mary Nell Lee

Ron and Dr. Ali Hassan in Cairo.

Randall Lee

The Sun Altar at Hatshepsut's mortuary temple.

He spent a great deal of time with us and nothing was withheld that I wanted to see. I had already been to these places but the additional freedom I was afforded to see whatever I wanted was beyond my wildest dreams. The main thing I wanted to see was the Solar Altar at Djeser Djeseru which I had not been able to see on previous trips.

But it was something else that made the entire trip unforgettable. After viewing the Solar Altar, I wandered into some doors that led to very dark areas. Dr. Hassan told me that area was not open to the public as it had not been restored. But he allowed me to look around.

This was before digital cameras and when I stuck my camera in those areas and took flash pictures, I had no idea what they would reveal until I returned home and had the film developed. I never really thought much about it when I took all the rolls of film to be developed.

When I saw the pictures, it took me a little while to remember where the photographs were taken since we went to so many different places. Then I remembered the darkened room, and for a minute, I lost my breath. There on the wall was a young girl in a procession with some gods and behind her, and a very odd looking goddess, was a young boy. I could think of nothing else this could represent except pharaoh's daughter with her adopted son, Moses. After all, this was Hatshepsut's mortuary temple and was devoted to her life.

Mary Nell Lee

Above in orange is figure of Hatshepsut. Following, seen below, is Senenmut (Moses).

Mary Nell Lee

I had never seen this before in all of the journals, articles and books I have scoured. Then while writing this book, I found the drawing of the scene obviously made many years ago when the temple was first discovered.

There was no information with the picture except the name of the file, "Amenophis and various goddesses inner sanctuary." "Amenophis" is the old spelling of Amenhotep. This name in Hatshepsut's mortuary temple provides the confirmation of her father also having the name Amenhotep in addition to Thutmose.

I firmly believe that it is depicting young Neferure with probably twelve year old Senenmut since that was his age when he came to the palace.

Senenmut built Thutmose I's Obelisks

Senenmut was in charge of many major projects on behalf of the throne. **He is known as the architect of Hatshepsut's mortuary temple, Djeser Djeseru.**

Another major project concerned the obelisks for Thutmose I's upcoming jubilee. Obelisks are mammoth sized, 4-sided narrow stone structures with vertical columns that taper slightly as they go upward. Inscriptions on the sides sometime indicate that their top pyramidion was covered in gold or electrum, which is a combination of silver and gold.

Only 6 remain in Egypt while perhaps as many as 22 are in different countries after being carted off as either gifts or plunder from invaders. The largest ever made were made during the 18th Dynasty.

The most amazing fact about a true obelisk is that it is made from one piece of stone. The ancient Egyptians would place them at the entrance to their temples or in the courtyard. Thutmose I had erected two of them in the early years of his reign.

One of these earlier obelisks made by Thutmose I is about 64 feet tall and is estimated to weigh 143 tons. The inscriptions mention his titles and that he made them as a monument to his father, Amun, meaning the god and not his literal father.

In Thutmose I's year 15, another pair was ordered to be made which were more spectacular than the first ones. Ineni, a high official of Thutmose I wrote about this second set of obelisks. In his biography on the walls of his tomb that he transported these obelisks:

"I inspected the erection of two obelisks------built the august boat of 120 cubits in its length, 40 cubits in its width in order to transport these obelisks. (They) came in peace, safety and prosperity, and landed at Karnak laid with every pleasant wood."

While Ineni was in charge of the inspection and transportation of these obelisks, it was Senenmut who was in charge of the actual quarrying, fashioning, inscribing and retrieval of those obelisks. These are the two obelisks that were to be erected for Hatshepsut's father's Sed Festival.

Randall Lee

One (of a pair) of the first obelisks erected by Thutmose I at Karnak.

Only one of Thutmose I's earlier obelisks remains standing in the court at Karnak between the Third and Fourth Pylons but the one remaining of this later pair surpasses it in size and weight. It is 94 feet tall and estimated to weigh 323 tons!

The following inscription, engraved on the rocks at Aswan, tells about Senenmut's involvement with the work of securing the two obelisks:

"Ascription of [honor] to the Divine Consort, Sovereign of the entire Two Lands, by the wearer of the royal seal, companion, great in love, chief steward, Senmut. Came the hereditary prince, count, who [greatly] satisfies the heart of the Divine Consort, who pleases the Mistress of the Two Lands by his injunction, chief steward of the Princess, Nefrure, who liveth, Senmut, in order to conduct the work of two great obelisks of a "Myriad-(of-years"). It took place according to that which was commanded; everything was done; it took place because of the fame of her majesty."

Mary Nell Lee

Thutmose I's earlier obelisk is at left. The taller one of the right is one of a pair erected in his honor by Hatshepsut for his Sed Festival.

It is interesting that in this rock engraving, Hatshepsut is referred to as Neferure, because soon the name "Neferure" would no longer be found in inscriptions. This proves that she used both names for a long time.

To verify that these are the obelisks built in honor of Thutmose I's jubilee of 30 years, or Sed Festival, the following is inscribed on one of them:

"Her majesty made the name of her father to be established in this monument perpetually, praise being made of the King of the South and the North, Akheperkara (Thotmose I) by the majesty of this god." ("Cleopatra's Needles and Other Egyptian Obelisks" by E. A. Wallis Budge, p. 103.)

On another side, it says:

"... which she made (i.e. dedicated) to him on the first day of the Set festival..." (Budge, p. 105)

The phrase "myriad of years" and "Set festival" in Senenmut's inscription above confirms the identity of the obelisks Senenmut was sent to obtain as being those for Thutmose I's Sed Festival. Work began in year 15 of Thutmose I (year 27 of his reign as Amenhotep I), allowing 3 years for them to be quarried, shaped, inscribed, brought to Thebes and finally erected in time for the Sed Festival. The obelisks were finished, delivered and erected two years prior to the time for the Sed Festival of Hatshepsut's father, Thutmose I, which probably made an impression on the pharaoh as to the abilities of young Senenmut.

The Sed Festival was a festival for a pharaoh who had attained thirty years on the throne. Going back to the early days of ancient Egypt, it was a festival designed as a renewal of the pharaoh's strength and confirm to the people that he was still healthy and able to rule. If a pharaoh continued to rule longer than 30 years, these festivals were held at three year intervals.

But scholars state that this Sed Festival (also called The Heb-Sed Festival) referred to on the obelisks is actually Hatshepsut's. This is not realistic. These festivals were very important to the pharaoh as well as to the people. A major misconception has completely confused an entire dynasty's history.

This is another instance where the given regnal year does not specify the pharaoh's name. At the time, I'm sure it wasn't needed because everyone knew who was the emperor pharaoh.

The general belief among scholars that future king Thutmose III is portrayed in Hatshepsut's mortuary temple in several instances really makes no sense concerning the early years of Hatshepsut's "reign." One instance is in the northwest hall of offerings where a scene portrays a king who is identified as Thutmose III offering to Amun. The inscription reads:

"(I) give to thee the celebrating of millions of Sed-festivals on the throne of Horus and that thou direct all the living like Re for ever."

This is an obvious reference to the Sed festival of Thutmose I.

The Wrong Thutmose Again

In the colonnade where Hatshepsut's birth scene and coronation are on the walls, some pillars of the colonnade are decorated with scenes of Thutmose I being embraced by Amun. Again I would like to stress that scholars have designated this as Thutmose III. However, I will reiterate, the name is written a little differently than Thutmose III would later write his name. It was translated "MenkheperKAre" instead of Menkheperre, which is how the future Thutmose III would later write his name.

Yet, it was decided long ago that this aberration in the name of Thutmose was the later pharaoh, Thutmose III instead of Thutmose I. Only when these instances in Hatshpesut's temple are attributed to her father do they make sense. The only reason this interpretation was accepted was because of earlier preconceived notions.

Other scenes in the colonnade with Thutmose I include Hatshepsut with inscriptions in connection with the Sed festival. This incorrect identification led to scholars declaring this proved that Hatshepsut shared a Sed festival with young Thutmose III instead of it referencing her father's Sed festival. I strongly propose this has caused confusion in the chronology of events. There are a number of scholars who have addressed this issue but all still accept the fact that it is Thutmose III in her life scenes in her temple. For example:

"Menkheperkara appears to be an early form of Thutmose's (III) prenomen, one which he subsequently abandoned. It does not appear to have been used on any of his later monuments dating from year twenty-two onwards." (Journal of Near Eastern Studies, Vo,l. 20, No. 4, "A Joint Sed-Festival of Thutmose III and Queen Hatshepsut," by E. P. Uphill, p. 250.)

Mary Nell Lee
Tomb 353 (TT353), the second tomb built for Senenmut.

Meanwhile, prior to the time for the pharaoh's Sed festival, other events were happening which looked as if something was about to occur.

A New Tomb for Senenmut

After year 16 of Thutmose I, there are no more mentions of the name Neferure or Senenmut on monuments or temple walls. It was a period of transition. In year 16 of Thutmose I when Moses was 27 years old, work began on this new tomb. This would have been considered his royal tomb.

TT358 is located just below Hatshepsut's mortuary temple in a location that shows his high favor with her and her father. This tomb was more in line with

Mary Nell Lee

The scene in Senemut's tomb 353 with his parents, Hatnofer and Ramose. This is the tomb that archaeologists remembered when they found their tomb. If they had not made the connection, Hatnofer and Ramose's tomb may never have received the attention it did.

Mary Nell Lee

Work stopped on the tomb in the middle of completion. The portion in black ink has not been carved into the rock.

a royal tomb, although throughout it, Senenmut is referred to as non-royal. His parents are also portrayed prominently in it and this was the tomb the excavators remembered when they found Moses' parent's tomb.

It is very eerie to go down into that tomb and see how, at the time Moses fled and gave up his claim to the future throne, all work stopped on this tomb and it remains exactly as it was left to this day. It is finished down to the lower section of hieroglyphs and pictures- then, where the workmen stopped work, the pictures are drawn onto the wall in black ink.

Equally amazing is the fact that, unlike other Egyptian tombs where the deceased is pictured with a wife and family, Moses is shown with only his mother and father, Hatnofer and Ramose, since he was never married while in Egypt.

The portrait of Senenmut found on the wall of the tomb is similar to the sketches found on rock shards below his first tomb 71. While there is not a great difference in this one and the earlier ones, he does appear a little more mature as he was 27 years old here.

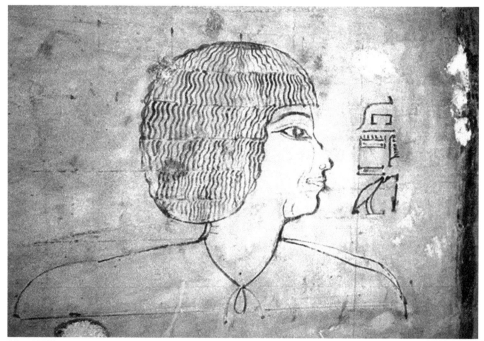

Mary Nell Lee

Above, the drawing of Senenmut inside his second tomb, number 353. His name is written next to it in heiroglyph.

Mary Nell Lee
A portion of the astronomical ceiling in Senenmut's tomb.

Metropolitan Museum of Art- CC0
A shard with a sketch of Senenmut from his earlier tomb 71. It appears as if the artists went to great effort to portray him accurately as is seen in the unique shape of his nose. This would have been a feature of his Hebrew race and he obviously wanted it recorded correctly.

There is an astronomical ceiling in Senenmut's tomb, the earliest ever known. The accuracy of the large diagram has led some scholars to place the date of this sky at either 1436 BC or 1534 BC. However, it has also been stated that it is not possible to give an accurate account of the date due to the great number of years since it was completed.

Recap of Who's Who in Chapter 9

Within the tombs built for Senenmut, his family is revealed and is entirely consistent with the Biblical account.

Senenmut was Moses, the son of Hatnofer (Biblical name Jochebed) and Ramose (Biblical name Amram).

His brother was Amenemhat (Biblical name Aaron) and his sister was Ahhotep (Biblical name Miriam). Amenemhat is depicted in his tomb 353 with Senenmut and Hatshepsut in chamber A.

There have been claims of evidence of other siblings of Senenmut, but they are not mentioned in his tombs which could mean, if he did have other siblings, that they had died.

Chapter 10

MOSES
HEIR TO THE THRONE

Tuthmosis II
Akheperenre

Moses Became Thutmose II

Year 18 of Thutmose I was when his Sed Festival was celebrated. It was the 30th year he had been a pharaoh, counting his years as Amenhotep I when he had been the co-regent in the northern capital of Memphis.

It was also regnal year 12 of Hatshepsut. A change had definitely taken place; Hatshepsut was now considered "the great royal wife, the king's sister, the king's mother." She was no longer called "king."

Through the legitimization of Hatshepsut, the path was provided for the young Hebrew to rise to the second highest position in the nation of Egypt, just as his ancestor Joseph had done.

In viewing the events of Moses' life in Egypt, I am impressed with the wisdom the pharaoh must have had. Although there are so many arguments over who did what, I believe Hatshepsut's father was extremely wise and chose extremely capable officials. It appears he was cautious with Moses as the inscriptions show a gradual rise in Senenmut's official life even though he did bear over 90 titles over the course of time. I believe Senenmut proved himself extremely worthy of all the positions even though it is obvious that at first he was given these because he was Hatshepsut's adopted son whom she obviously loved greatly.

The year of the emperor's Jubilee or Heb-Sed Festival according to his years as Amenhotep I, was the year Thutmose I officially elevated Moses to the position of Thutmose II.

Although information is scarce, it appears that Moses remained in Thebes rather than moving to Memphis. The indication is that he would take the throne as emperor upon his adopted grandfather's death. For the time being he was obviously still under the care and oversight of the pharaoh and pharaoh's daughter. And, as we will soon discuss, another young man would be chosen as his co-regent.

There is not a great deal known of his time as Thutmose II. We know that the names Senenmut disappeared from the records as did the name Neferure. It is known that the Egyptian army continued to mount expeditions to quell uprisings in Nubia and they conquered the Kushite kingdom of Kerma.

A rock-cut stele inscription at Aswan dated to Thutmose II regnal year 1 is the only date of his reign I have been able to find documented. It describes an uprising in Kush that resulted in the death of all the enemies except for the son of the ruler. This son was brought back to Egypt as a hostage and this effectively ended any problems with them.

It is extremely important to examine every scrap of data we can find concerning Thutmose II. The common belief of scholars and Egyptologists is that one pharaoh took the throne only after the earlier one had died, but this idea is not what the evidence reveals. The following inscription of Thutmose II is very important as it proves that Thutmose I was still alive during Thutmose II's year 1:

Year I, second month of the first season, day 8, coronation day under the majesty of Horus: Mighty Bull, Powerful in Strength; Favorite of the Two Goddesses: Divine in kingship; Golden Horus: Powerful in Being; King of Upper and Lower Egypt: Okhepernere, Son of Re: Thutmose (II), …

*One came to inform his majesty as follows: " The wretched Kush has begun to rebel, those who were under the dominion of the 'Lord of the Two Lands' purpose hostility, beginning to smite him. The inhabitants of Egypt are about to bring away the cattle behind this fortress which thy father built in his campaigns, the King of Upper and Lower Egypt, Okheperkere (Thutmose I), **living forever;**… …The King of Upper and Lower Egypt: Okhepernere, Son of Re: Thutmose (II) Beautiful in Diadems, given life, stability, satisfaction, like Re, forever.* ("Ancient Records of Egypt, Vol. II" by Henry Breasted, pp 48-9.)

The reference to Okheperkere (Thutmose I), followed by "living forever" proves that he was living at this time. I suspect this belief that one king died then another came to the throne is because of the weight given to the tomb biographies of Ineni and Ahmose-Pen-Nekhbet, among others, who list the kings they served under, stating that each one arose when the previous one flew to heaven or died. For example, Ineni recalled his service under Thutmose I and has Thutmose II come to the throne at his death:

"The king rested from life, going forth to heaven, having completed his years in gladness of heart. The Hawk in the nest [appeared as] the King of Upper and Lower Egypt, Okhepernere (C'-bpr-n-R C, Thutmose II), he became king of the Black Land and ruler of the Red Land, having taken possession of the Two Regions in triumph." (Breasted, p. 47)

Yet, the above stele at Aswan proves Thutmose I and Thutmose II were both alive during the rebellion of Nubia and Kush.

Ahmose-Pen-Nekhbet gives the only record of a campaign into Asia by Thutmose II although it doesn't give a date:

"I followed King Okhepernere (Thutmose II), triumphant; there were brought off for me in Shasu very many living prisoners; I did not count them. [Gifts which were brought to] the fame of the king, Okhepernere (Thutmose II) [from his vic] tories -------- elephant[s] ----- horse[s] ----- [Retenu] the Upper -------- [the land] of Niy ----- kings ----- his majesty in ----- [when] he came out of -----." (Breasted p 51.)

The subject of Thutmose II has proven to be a mystery to the scholars and archaeologists who are stumped by the fact that no tomb for him has ever been found. I propose the answer to that question is that he chose to have his tomb in his name of Senenmut, the son of Hatnofer and Ramose, instead of a traditional royal tomb. The only thing known for sure is Thutmose II suddenly disappeared from recorded history just as Senenmut did.

I propose that all the statues and scenes on temple walls depicting Hatshepsut as a male "king" were intended to be changed to reflect the name of Moses when he became co-regent and finally the emperor pharaoh. The evidence as I view it appears as a well laid out plan from the beginning.

In "The Thutmosid Succession" by William F. Edgerton, the author reviewed all the available data pertaining to the theory that Thutmose III was responsible for changing a large number of Hatshepsut's inscriptions and cartouches to those of both her father, Thutmose I, and Thutmose II. He is attempting to provide a correct chronology of the reigns of Thutmose II, Hatshepsut and Thutmose III. It is a painful presentation of the many arguments among the early scholars who set the stage for the commonly accepted historical scheme.

To try to understand the issues, the author, who was living in Luxor in the service of the Oriental Institute of the University of Chicago, personally journeyed to examine many of the instances of disputed or misunderstood inscriptions concerning changes made. What he relates in his paper supports my belief that Hatshepsut's cartouches as "king" were intended to be changed to the name of Thutmose II when Moses assumed that position.

When discussing inscriptions on the walls of Hathsepsut's Hathor Temple at Deir el-Bahri, specifically the inner sanctuary, room E, he wrote:

"Hatshepsut was original everywhere in one place on each of the two long walls (the north and south walls), where an original Thutmose III still kneels behind her. Her pictures seem untouched; her cartouches were all erased, but usually so lightly that all signs are still clearly legible. Substitutions seems to have been made, in paint, only in all of the erased cartouches; and a number of horizontal lines suggestive of ( ) and traces suggesting the name Thutmose

limit the substituted names in general to Thutmose I and II. In only one case can I decide between the two, namely on the north wall just behind the cow's horns (unpublished). .... This one cartouche, at least, was appropriated for Thutmose II; the other cartouches of Hatshepsut were probably appropriated either for him or for Thutmose I." ("The Thutmosid Succession" by William F. Edgerton, pages 11 and 12.)

His paper is highly technical and assumes the reader is familiar with hieroglyphics but is straightforward with his description of the evidences and what he believes they mean. He presents the different theories of different scholars as to why Hatshepsut's name was erased and replaced by Thutmose II's name. One theory he presents is that this may have been done by the 19th Dynasty, but he quickly disregards that idea:

"The argument is essentially that only a few of the greatest pharaohs (notably Thutmose III) made such an impression on posterity that later kings were moved to perpetuate their names- and then only under very special circumstances, perhaps only in cases where the dead king had had some actual connection, direct or indirect, with the monument on which his name was later inserted; that the insertion of the name of such an insignificant ruler as Thutmose II by any later king on a monument which was not begun until after Thutmose II's death, and without any phrase naming the actual author of the insertion, would be totally unparalleled." (Edgerton, page. 25.)

Mention is also made of several original representations of the names of Thutmose I and Thutmose II on the walls of the temple of Beuhen, which is evidence that Thutmose I lived much longer than is accepted.

The truth is the evidence available is not a complete picture of events. We can only piece it together based on our core beliefs of the situation in Egypt during that time. As each piece of evidence became known, I had to evaluate it in light of Ron's theory. More and more, it came together in a coherent view of the life of Moses in pharaoh's court with his adopted mother.

The issue of the innumerable cartouches containing the royal name of Hatshepsut being changed to another name is one of the reasons I believe there are so many different theories concerning Hatshepsut proclaiming herself "king." The main theory is that Thutmose III was mad at her and tried to erase her memory. Thutmose III will be discussed soon but I found no evidence that this occurred. I stand by my stance that her name on statues was intended to be changed to Moses' royal name in due time.

What Did Moses Look Like?

Some evidences were found in and near Senenmut's two tombs, tomb 71 and tomb 353 which were discussed earlier. There is one unique feature to these sketches- the person is portrayed with a unique shape to the bridge of his nose. It has a bit of a curve rather than a straight line, a small hump if you want to call it that.

This is a feature which I believe was unique to Moses in the Egyptian capitol and was purposefully used. It was a feature of his Hebrew race. I found this feature on no other Egyptian statues portraying pharaohs other than those I believe were originally of Moses but were usurped by other kings.

Statues of Senenmut present images of Moses when he was a young man. This is evidenced when they are viewed as some even appear to be of a teenager. The quality of these statues, while good, is not as refined as future statues.

Also Senenmut makes the claim that he designed the cryptogram of Hatshepsut's royal name, seen on his statues. The cryptogram of Hatshepsut

Both photos this page- Randall Lee

Senenmut statue in the Kimbell Museum in Ft. Worth, Texas.

Mary Nell Lee

Left and above- Statue of Senenmut in the Brooklyn Museum in New York City. Although the statue is similar in design to the one on the previous page, he looks older. He is perhaps 16 to 18 years old.

Mary Nell Lee

is the design of hieroglyphs forming the name Maatkare, seen on the statues at left and above.

The statue of Senenmut on the previous page is in the Kimbell Museum in Ft. Worth, Texas. The unique shape of his nose is evident. Whenever I had the privilege of examining statues in person that I believed were representing Moses, I carefully examined the nose.

The Kimbell Museum statue on the previous page may be the youngest representation of Moses other than the statues of him as a baby in young Neferure's arms. Seen from a different angle, he looks as if he could be as young as 12 or 14 years old. The statue from the Brooklyn Museum, which is the same type of pose, depicts him a little older, perhaps 16 or 18 years old. While the ancient Egyptians had a formula for every aspect of art, whether a statue or on a wall, it is evident that certain features are carefully preserved which are unique to the individual being portrayed. The statues of Moses are all identifiable. He not only had the unique shape to his nose, his face seemed to beam. He was a very handsome man.

Mary Nell Lee

Above- Some of the many statue heads from Hatshepsut's mortuary temple. They are said to represent Hatshepsut.

Mary Nell Lee

Mary Nell Lee

Above- Statue head, also from Hatshepsut's temple, is in the Cairo Museum. It is also said to represent Hatshepsut. As explained, I believe all of these were made in the image of Moses and all would have been changed to his name when he ascended to the throne.

 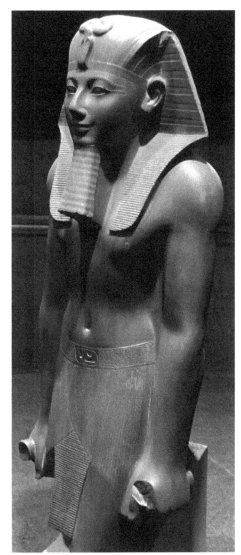

Clint Loveness *Randall Lee*

Statue usurped by Thutmose III that was originally Moses in the Luxor Museum.

The above statue in the Luxor Museum has the cartouche of Thutmose III on the belt. However, I believe this is definitely a statue made of Moses in preparation for when he became the emperor. When we examine statues of Thutmose III, the fact this does not depict him becomes evident. That, added to the fact it looks so much like the other statues said to be Hatshepsut, make it unlikly to be Thutmose III and extremely likely to be Moses.

Right-Thutmose III statue that is actually Moses in the Cairo Museum. See next page for better view from the side. This was obviously made when he was a mature man.

Different scholars have noted it is difficult, if not impossible, to identify a statue as being either Hatshesput or Thutmose III due to the fact many of them are so similar. Some have gone so far as to note minute distinctions which denote one from the other, such as a narrower chin, or propose that it makes sense for them to look similar since they are related.

But there is no evidence that Thutmose III is related to Hatshepsut. That idea comes from the notion that all pharaohs are the son of the previous pharaoh. Thutmose III, as will be shown later, would have had no need for the story he recorded of his selection by the god to be the pharaoh if he was legally in line to the throne.

Finally, the statue on this page and the next is my favorite and was one of the first I ever saw in person. It is in the Cairo Museum and the magnificence of this statue surpasses any other I have ever seen in spite of it being damaged. This one is another statue with the name Thutmose III on it and I am absolutely convinced that this is one of the last statues made of Moses.

Many statues of pharaohs have been found without the name on them. This leads to the obvious conclusion that statues were made in anticipation of the man's ascent to the throne. In Moses' case, he fled before he was able to take the throne as the emperor pharaoh. The pharaoh who took his place had a wealth of statues to choose from.

Mary Nell Lee

Dating and Timeline Recap

To recap the dating of the dynasty, Manetho gave Ahmose 25 years and 4 months and Thutmose I 12 years. In my timeline, 12 years is how long Thutmose I ruled by the name of Amenhotep I as co-regent for his father, Ahmose. However, the old pharaoh, Thutmose I, was still alive when Moses fled according to the Bible. So his reign lasted at least 29 years and that is provided he died the same year Moses fled. These dates are based on the only dates recorded in his name. Many did not mention his name as discussed.

I will present evidence that he most likely died in his 31st year of his reign, two years after Moses fled. This is a case, I believe, where no dated monuments or inscriptions are known of his latter years so he is believed to have died much earlier than he actually did. In reality, in preparing for the next monarch, the years of Hatshepsut and Thutmose II were recorded visibly by the old pharaoh to establish them in the dynasty.

Manetho gives Amenhotep I 20 years and 7 months which ends close to the time the regnal years of Hatshepsut begin. I show her regnal years beginning in his 19th year. Again, as he is the same person as Thutmose I, I believe he died in his regnal year 43. While these sound like a long number of years for a pharaoh to rule, if he came to the throne at age 30 then he would be in his early 70's when he died.

To briefly address the issue of Amenhotep I and Thutmose I and their regnal dates, I found that there was nothing known to firmly establish a complete timeline. Thutmose I recorded more in his Thutmosid name than in his Amenhotep name.

Manetho lists Hatshepsut as having a 21 year and 9 month reign. I show in the timeline how her regnal years ended sometime in year 22 which is a perfect fit. The fact that so many dates were recorded of her reign as the heir apparent to the throne adds credence to the idea that Thutmose I paid more attention to establishing her to ensure the throne was secure.

Chapter 11

MOSES FLED EGYPT

This is a major event in the Biblical record. The implication of the statue and inscription records is that right up until the time Moses fled, he was secure in his position as the next emperor pharaoh by being fully accepted by both his adopted grandfather and adopted mother. This gives added impetus to Moses' fear of the pharaoh learning that he had killed an Egyptian who was mistreating a Hebrew slave.

Exo 2:11 And it came to pass in those days, when Moses was grown, that he went out unto his brethren, and looked on their burdens: and he spied an Egyptian smiting an Hebrew, one of his brethren. 12 And he looked this way and that way, and when he saw that there was no man, he slew the

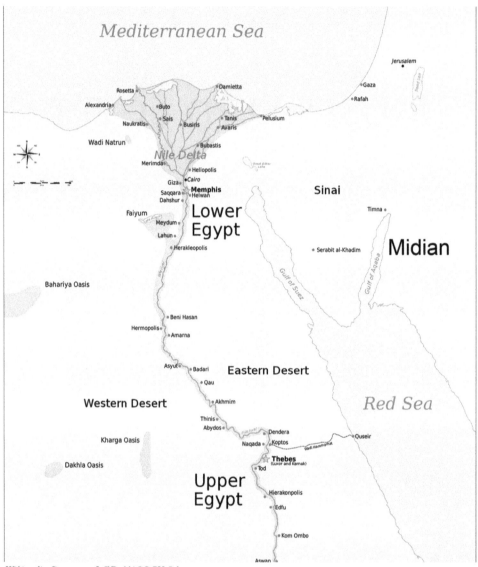

Wikimedia Commons- Jeff Dahl/ CC BY-SA

Egyptian, and hid him in the sand. 13 And when he went out the second day, behold, two men of the Hebrews strove together: and he said to him that did the wrong, Wherefore smitest thou thy fellow? 14 And he said, Who made thee a prince and a judge over us? intendest thou to kill me, as thou killedst the Egyptian? And Moses feared, and said, Surely this thing is known. 15 Now when Pharaoh heard this thing, he sought to slay Moses. But Moses fled from the face of Pharaoh, and dwelt in the land of Midian…

Moses was visiting northern Egypt when he went out to see his brethren, the children of Israel, because the Delta region in the north is where they lived. We don't know if the pharaoh, his adopted grandfather, had come to Memphis with him or not but I would propose he remained in Thebes. He was elderly by now and wouldn't have made the trip unless it was completely necessary. But I don't know. All we are told is that Moses feared the pharaoh's reaction and fled.

The situation in Egypt for the royal family and government members would have been one of confusion, anger and sadness when Moses left out of fear of the pharaoh. Hatshepsut's heart was surely broken. The pharaoh was furious but I imagine he was also sad. We don't know if Moses had an opportunity to tell Hatshepsut good-bye or not.

What we do know is that Egypt, much like the British monarchy of today, kept a stiff upper lip and said nothing. There was nothing ill said publicly about Thutmose II according to ancient records that have survived. He was considered, at the least, the embodiment of the god Toth. It is likely that the pharaoh never allowed the true story to be known to the people. It would have been an affront to the god Toth and it was probably also a very great humiliation to the royal family.

Moses knew the country and the area well. He took his journey across the Sinai Peninsula, then along the northern edge of the Gulf of Aqaba arm of the Red Sea. He then turned south and went to Midian. All of Egypt and the troops stationed in Canaan, Syria and Lebanon to the north would most certainly have recognized him or at least known who he was.

Moses had spent the last 28 years in the palace where flattery and praise were heaped upon him. He could do no wrong. He knew no want. He believed he was to be the deliverer of his people but he didn't wait for God to direct his steps. It was clearly not God's plan to deliver His people through warfare. It is impossible to imagine what went through Moses' mind as he journeyed to this foreign land where he probably knew no one.

Handling the Loss of the Future King

When Moses fled, there was again a problem- no one to take the throne after Hatshepsut's father died. If Thutmose I had been 30 years old when he came to throne, he was now 71, still a feasible age for a pharaoh to be alive and in reasonable health.

Judging from the photograph of the wall in Djeser-Djeseru that I took in the 1990s which showed a young girl with a younger boy, I would suggest that Hatshepsut was at the most, 12- 14 years older than Moses. This would mean she was a young teenager when she rescued Moses and would have been at the most 54 years old when he fled.

Thutmose II (Moses) Portrayed as Dead

William Edgerton described a very interesting scene on the two long walls of the 1st sanctuary room where both Hathsepsut's father, Thutmose I, and Thutmose II are characterized as "justified in the presence of the Great God," which simply means they are deceased. Accompanied by other deceased family members, they are shown walking from the west (abode of the dead) to the Bark of Amun. I propose this as evidence the royal family handled the desertion of Moses (Thutmose II) by presenting him as dead. This would have limited the humiliation of the king and Hatshesput and kept the truth from the public.

As I write this, the world around us in the United States has erupted into a frenzy, trying to eliminate evidence of history that offends different people. Statues are being pulled down and destroyed. It is not a new idea for some civilizations to attempt to control their perceived history.

In ancient Egypt, the memory of Thutmose II was never attacked. There are few records but the perceived picture by scholars is that he was a sickly and weak man who died early. But in the whole scheme of things, a different scenario emerges.

Thutmose III was to be Moses' Co-Regent

Pharaoh Thutmose I had not left the nation exposed to a possible empty throne. There was young man in Memphis who had already been selected to be the co-regent for Moses. The evidence indicates that he had been appointed to the office of co-regent the year before Moses fled which indicates that the time was getting near for Moses' elevation to the position of senior pharaoh. The old pharaoh most likely knew his time was nearing.

The plan implemented to raise Moses to the throne through Hatshepsut was now used to place this young man in his position. It is not possible to determine how long Hatshepsut was his regent. But we do know he was young at that time. When he became Amenhotep II, he left an inscription which told how he came to the throne at the age of 18.

Wikimedia Commons– Louvre Museum/ Public Domain

Tuthmosis III
Menkheperre

When he was appointed co-regent, Thutmose III began his regnal year dating at year 22 of Hatshepsut's regnal years, most likely to provide continuity. It is a unique situation as he wasn't even born yet in year 1 of Hatshepsut's reign. In his regnal year 54, he was only 50 or 51. This is also a cause of great confusion.

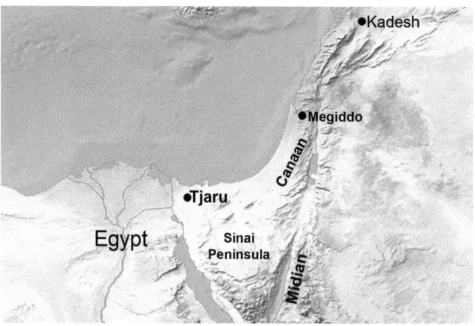

Wikimedia Commons- Natural Earth/ CC BY-SA

The evidence indicates right before Moses fled Egypt, arrangements were being made for the next generation to rule the united Egypt and Thutmose III was appointed as co-regent in preparation for Moses' final ascension to the throne which couldn't occur until Thutmose I/Amenhotep I died.

Under Thutmose I, Egypt had lived in peace and prosperity. Inscriptions show Moses, as Thutmose II, was not heavily involved in military expansion although he did participate in campaigns when needed. After the expulsion of the Hyksos, Egypt was keen to keep them out of Egypt. They settled in Canaan, Syria and Lebanon. Egypt had stationed troops throughout the region to keep them as vassals.

The Warrior Pharaoh

All was calm for a while, but when Thutmose III was appointed as Thutmose II's co-regent in year 22, he immediately left on his first military campaign to Megiddo to handle a serious uprising. When the newly appointed Thutmose III headed off to war, he left Memphis and mustered his troops at Tjaru. The fortress there served as an armory with all the weapons and other outfitting needed for an army.

The leader of the uprising was the Prince of Kadesh followed by 330 rulers of city-states. But not all vassals were involved in the uprising. Thutmose III's Armant Stele told how he *"didn't halt while proceeding to the land of Djahi, to slay the rebels who were there and give goods to those who were loyal to him."*

The entire campaign is recorded in great detail in his Annals on the inside walls of the Karnak Temple of Amun. His siege there lasted 7 or 8 months where he was overwhelmingly successful. He recorded that some of the princes were set free after the battle and siege were over and that they left *"on donkeys for I had seized their chariotry".*

He also took some of the children and wives of the rulers of countries who had been part of the coalition that had fought against Egypt. Those people were taken as *"living prisoners"* to *"fill the workhouse of his father Amun in Karnak."*

In his Annals, he tells of his great military expertise, as when approaching Megiddo and his army officers expressed concern about taking a narrow pass. The pharaoh wrote of his decision:

"Then his majesty commanded the entire army [to march] -- [upon] that road which threatened to be [narrow. His ma.jesty] swore, saying: 'None shall go forth in the way before my majesty, in--- .' He went forth at the head of his army himself, showing [the way by his (own) footsteps; horse behind [horse], his majesty being at the head of his army." (Breasted, p. 181)

During the battle:

"Then his majesty prevailed against them at the head of his army, and when they saw his majesty prevailing against them they fled headlong to Megiddo (-My-k-ty) in fear, abandoning their horses and their chariots of gold and silver. The peopled hauled them (up), pulling (them) by their clothing, into this city; the people of this city having closed (it) against them [and lowered clothing to pull them up into this city. Now, if only the army of his majesty had not given their heart to plundering the things of the enemy, they would have [captured] Megiddo (My-k-ty) at this moment, when the wretched foe of (Kd-J) Kadesh and the wretched foe of this city were hauled up in haste to bring them into this city. The fear of his majesty had entered [their hearts], their arms were powerless, his serpent diadem was victorious among them." (Breasted p. 184)

The mention of the people lowering clothing to pull them up into the city reminded me of the Biblical story of Rahab. Joshua had sent two spies into Jericho and Rahab took them into her house to stay. But then the king of

Thutmose III's Battle of Megiddo relief at the 7th Pylon in Karnak

Jericho heard about the spies and told Rahab to bring them to him. Instead, she hid them on the roof of her house in bundles of stalks of flax and finally:

JOS. 2:15 Then she let them down by a cord through the window; for her house was upon the wall, and she dwelt upon the wall.

In the list of booty gained from this defeat were 924 chariots among other things. Listed is the chariot of the Prince of Kadesh which was of gold. Then he mentions *"their chariots of gold and silver were made spoil;"*

In reading of his exploits, if they seem too good to be true, remember that Alexander the Great conquered the entire known world and died at age 32.

Hatshepsut's Father Died

In Thutmose III's year 25, the old pharaoh, Thutmose I died. In the two years between the time Moses fled and Thutmose I died, Thutmose III proved himself more than capable of ruling by virtue of his great victory at Megiddo. Thutmose I most certainly gave his blessing to this young man's ascension to the throne before he died.

Although Hatshepsut was his regent for awhile, beginning with year 22 of her reign when he was first appointed, doesn't mean she told him what to do. It was only a legal means to the throne. He appeared to have a very good relationship with her despite all the books and papers which talk about how he hated her and launched a campaign to remove her memory from the monuments about his year 42. I disagree that this was the reason for any of the changes made on monuments.

When he came of age, Hatshepsut's name ceased to be associated with his. Although I cannot identify the exact year this occurred, I believe it happened when he became the emperor in his year 25 when he was 21 years old. (Remember, he absorbed into his regnal years the years of Hatshepsut and he wasn't born until 4 years later). But indications are that he remained in a good relationship with her.

He later wanted his legacy to show that he owed his emperorship to the god, Amun. After all, he had not been Hatshepsut's adopted son, the person through whom the process of attaining the throne through Hatshepsut had been devised.

As a result, in his year 42, Thutmose III had the story inscribed on a wall of the Karnak temple telling how he was chosen personally by the god Amun to be the king. The story goes that on the occasion of a great feast, the young future Thutmose III stood aside all the other young "priests in training" of the god Amun in Memphis. The statue of the god was then carried around until it stopped in front of him. He then continues to tell how the god chose him to be upon the throne:

"-------my ---- is he; I am his son, whom he commanded that I should be upon his throne, while I was one dwelling in his nest; he begat me in uprightness of heart there is no lie therein; since my majesty was a stripling, while I was a youth in his temple, before occurred my installation to be prophet my majesty. I was in the capacity of the "Pillar of his Mother," like the youth Horus in Khemmis. I was standing in the northern hypostyle -------------....

------------ [the god] made the circuit of the hypostyle on both sides of it, the heart of those who were in front did not comprehend his actions, while searching for my majesty in every place. On recognizing me, lo, he halted --------- [I threw myself on] the pavement, I prostrated myself in his presence. He set me before his majesty, I was stationed at the "Station of the King." He was astonished at me ------------ without untruth. Then they [revealed] before the people the secrets in the hearts of the gods, who know these his -------; there was none who knew them, there was none who revealed them [beside him].

He opened [for] me the doors of heaven; he opened the portals of the horizon of Re. I flew to heaven as a divine hawk, beholding his form in heaven; I adored his majesty -------------- feast. I saw the glorious forms of the Horizon-God upon his mysterious ways in heaven.

Re himself established me, I was dignified with the diadems which [we]re upon his head, his serpent-diadem, rested upon "[my forehead] ----------- [he satisfied] me with all his glories; I was sated with the counsels of the gods, like Horus, when he counted his body at the house of my father, Amon-Re. I was [present]ed with the dignities of a god, with my diadems." (Breasted pp. 59-61.)

This story established him indelibly in history as pharaoh in his own right by personal selection of the god. If he had been a legal heir and related to the pharonic family, he would not have needed such a story.

Thutmose III was from Memphis and as a military man, Memphis was the logical location to base his war efforts. To go south, it was easy to take a ship up the Nile. To go north, where he focused a great deal of his campaigns, he needed to be in the northern capitol. The main border fortress of Tjaru was where he would muster his troops and prepare to go to Canaan and beyond.

During the reign of Hatshepsut's father, Thutmose I, Egypt gained great wealth from the tribute given by Nubia and the southern countries that had been subdued and pacified as well as tribute from the countries he conquered in Syria and Canaan. Gold was plentiful as well as precious stone. There was relative peace after the expulsion of the Hyksos back to Canaan and Syria and an Egyptian presence was established throughout the region.

But in time, they began to rebel which is when Thutmose III began his campaigns, three years prior to the death of Thutmose I, which was during year 11 of Thutmose II.

Before Thutmose III's reign was ended, he expanded control of the Egyptian empire all the way from the Euphrates to the north to Sudan in the south. He was a great warrior, a great king and remained quiet about his personal life for he left little information in the records. But his Annals record his military exploits from year 22 through year 42, the most detailed account of a pharaoh's military career in Egyptian history.

It is only when we consider the Biblical account that the Hand of Divinity can be seen in the people and events of ancient history. It seems apparent that the God of Abraham was raising Egypt to unimaginable status and wealth in preparation for the events that lay ahead.

Emperor Amenhotep II

Wikimedia Commons– Anagoria/ CC BY

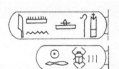

Amenhotep II
Akheperure

Wikimedia Commons- rivertay/ CC BY
Scene from Amenhotep's Amada Temple which shows both Amenhotep II and Thutmose III in equal positions in the same scene.

Thutmose III Became Emperor Amenhotep II

Three years after his appointment as Thutmose III, the old Pharaoh Thutmose I, Hatshepsut's father, died. Thutmose III then took on the additional title of Amenhotep II and became the emperor. Like Thutmose I, he continued to document most of his accomplishments in his Thutmose III name although he left records in his Amenhotep name as well.

Under Thutmose III's rule, the government grew as the wealth poured into the country in the form of booty from conquests and tribute from established relations. By now, the great wealth of Egypt was beyond comprehension. Egypt had become a world power like none other under Thutmose III. He was a military genius and brought much of the known world under Egypt's vassalship.

He left stelae and statues promoting his physical strength and abilities. Canaan was reduced to a vassal state. Troops were stationed in all the major cities. He was the perfect picture of what a pharaoh was expected to be. He was not shy and retiring and made great boasts of his physical prowess.

Evidence in support of the proposal that Thutmose III and Amenhotep II are the same king is provided in the above Amada relief which shows the

Randall Lee
Stele of Amenhotep II in the Luxor Museum.

king in both positions in the same scene. It simply was not the practice of pharaohs to include another king on their monuments or statues. Especially considering this king's ego, I propose that he is here promoting himself in both his Thutmose name and his Amenhotep name.

This Amada Temple in Nubia was built by this king and later a roof was added by the next pharaoh. For this reason scholars have stated this temple was begun by Thutmose III and Amenhotep II, as two separate individuals then work was continued by the next pharaoh. But the scene above does not reflect additional work as the scene was made as a single work.

In his Amenhotep II name, he left an inscription on his Sphinx stele which tells of his youth when he came to the throne:

"Now his Majesty appeared as king as a fine youth after he had become well developed, and had completed eighteen years in his strength and bravery,..."

A beautifully carved stele in the Museum at Luxor, seen above, contains the name of Amenhotep II and portrays him in his carriage with four-spoked wheels shooting arrows through a copper shield. This was a special area of boast for him as can be read in a portion of the Armant Stele written in his Thutmose III name:

"Year 22, second month of the Season of Growing, day 10. A summary of the deeds of valour and strength that this good god performed consisting of every excelling deed of bravery since the beginning of the first generation, which the lord of the gods, the lord of Armant, did for him, magnifying his victories to let his valour be related for millions of years to come, next to the deeds of bravery that His Majesty did continuously. If one were to recount a deed by its name, they would be too numerous to put into writing. When he shoots at a copper target, all wood is splintered like a papyrus reed. His Majesty offered an example thereof in the temple of Amun, with a target of hammered copper of three digits in thickness; when he had shot his arrow there, he caused protrusion of three palms behind it, so as to cause the followers to pray for the proficiency of his arms in valour and strength. I'm telling you what he did, without deception and without lie, in front of his entire army, and there is no word of exaggeration therein. When he spent a moment of recreation, hunting in any foreign land, the quantity that he captured was greater than what the entire army achieved. He slew seven lions by shooting in an instant. He captured a herd of twelve wild bulls in an hour at the time of breakfast, their tails behind him. He killed 120 elephants in the foreign country of Niya when he came from Naharina." (Translated by Mark-Jan Nederhof.)

In his Karnak stele, he tells of a rebellion in Syria and how he brought back the wives and children of the princes of those involved, the same thing recorded in his Thutmose III name. One of the things he chose to document in his imperial name, Amenhotep II, was his physical prowess, just as he did in his Thutmose III title. He was not shy when it came to extolling himself. In his Elephantine Stele dated to his year 4, it states:

"…great in strength, whose like does not exist; of whom a second is not found. He is a king very weighty of arm; there is not one who can draw his bow among his army among the hill-country sheiks (or) among the princes of Retenu, because his strength is so much greater than (that of) any king who has ever existed; raging like a panther, when he courses through the battlefield; there is none fighting before him; an archer mighty in smiting; a wall protecting Egypt;" (Breasted, p. 310)

He bragged of how he brought back seven princes hanging heads down on the prow of his barge from the Asiatic battle and his gruesome record of the events shows him to be ruthless:

"When his majesty returned with joy of heart to his father, Amon, he slew with his own weapon the seven princes, who had been in the district of Tikhsi (Ty-b-sy), and had been placed head downward at the prow of his majesty's barge, the name of which was: 'Okheprure (Amenhotep II)-is-the-Establisher-of-the-Two-Lands.' One hanged the six men of those fallen ones, before the wall of Thebes; those hands likewise. Then the other fallen one was taken up-river to Nubia and hanged on the wall of Napata (Npt), in order to cause to be manifest the victories of his majesty,…" (Breasted, p. 313)

During his reign, he led 16 or 17 military expeditions during a 20 year period. On the wall recording his Annals, he listed 350 cities he captured during his reign. The advanced technology gleaned from the Hyksos made it possible for the army to have the most advanced weaponry possible.

In his 33rd year, he attacked the Mitanni kingdom which had a large and powerful army. He took pontoon boats on oxcarts across Syria in order to cross the Euphrates. His great victory resulted in his bringing back to Egypt 30 members of the Mitanni king's harem and several hundred captured soldiers. He erected a stele on the bank of the Euphrates commemorating his victory next to Thutmose I's stele. On his journey home he stopped in the Orontes valley for an elephant hunt.

Wife and Royal Harem

Thutmose III had a royal wife by the name of Satiah who is mentioned in only a few places. He dedicated a statue of her after her death in the temple of Montu. But not much else is know about her.

He also began the practice of taking foreign wives. They may have actually been members of his harem rather than considered wives. The burial of three foreign princesses was found in a single tomb in a remote valley southwest of the Valley of the Kings. All three had been equipped alike with gold sandals, gold crowns, mirrors, two silver vases, a gold cup, a gold mounted alabaster kohl pot and all had their fingers and toes encased in gold sheaths. These things are all in addition to a large number of other articles.

Metropolitan Museum of Art   *Metropolitan Museum of Art*

A diadem and rosettes to be worn over a wig found in the tomb of the three foreign princesses at the Metropolitan Museum of Art.

Menhet, Menwi and Merti were obviously foreign and there is the very interesting theory that they were all buried at the same time due to the highly inaccessible location of the tomb.

The names of the women have been determined to be Semetic which most likely means they were wives or daughters of foreign chieftains he had conquered in his early wars in the regions of Canaan, Lebanon and Syria. There were items associated with this tomb with the name of Hatshepsut on them which proves Hatshepsut was still honored as royalty by Thutmose III.

An important fact to remember is that Thutmose III/Amenhotep II knew Moses personally. He was such a successful general that he came to be known as the Napolean of Egypt. As soon as he obtained the title of co-regent, he immediately left for battle. I am quite sure this was not something he did without the permission and full knowledge of the old pharaoh, Thutmose I.

He would have also known the true story of Moses and how he, as Thutmose II, fled the country after killing an Egyptian and burying him in the sand. This must be kept in mind as we recall the words of God when He was about to send Moses back to Egypt after 40 years in Midian:

*Exo. 4:19 And the LORD said unto Moses in Midian, Go, return into Egypt: for **all the men are dead which sought thy life.***

This king elevated Egypt to the heights of the greatest world power to date. All indications were that he was a brilliant military strategist and also possessed political abilities which managed the affairs of the country with great wisdom.

The more I have studied this young man, the more I am in awe of him. When viewed through the lens of the Biblical account, it appears that God placed the person on the throne He wanted there at this exact time.

A Co-Regent Appointed when Amenhotep I Died

When Thutmose III became emperor with the additional name of Amenhotep II, a co-regent was appointed at the same time. The new co-regent, Thutmose IV, was also a native of Memphis and again, we know little of his life prior to coming to the throne.

Like Thutmose III, he was not a member of the royal family and appeared to have come to the throne at an early age. His records tell of military campaigns but nothing on the order of those carried out by Thutmose III.

Since pharaohs don't usually mention anyone but themselves in their official records of events on temple walls and stelae, it is possible that he was on expeditions with the emperor, Amenhotep II. But it is also possible that the Egyptians did not allow both co-regent and emperor on the same military expedition in case of a defeat, leaving a void on the throne. I suggest, based on evidence, that Thutmose IV was quelling rebellions in the south while the emperor was on another important military exploit to the north.

I have noticed a preference for the pharaohs up to this point to prefer their "Thutmose" title over their "Amenhotep" name. However, that will change with this pharaoh.

It has been the practice down through the ages to assume each pharaoh was the son of the previous one. But I don't believe that to be possible for this king for the same reason as the previous pharaoh. He had a story explaining his rise to the throne, something that wouldn't be needed if he was the legal heir.

Like Thutmose III, his story tells of a god choosing him personally but his story has an added twist. In his "Dream Stele" erected between the paws of the Great Sphinx, he tells of a dream he had. He was resting in the shadow of the Sphinx when he fell asleep and had a dream.

In his dream, Harmachis, the god represented by the Sphinx, told him he would elevate him to the throne if he would free him from the sand which almost completely covered him. Part of the ending text is missing, but we know how the story ends since he became the pharaoh:

"One of those days it came to pass that the king's-son, Thutmose, came, coursing at the time of midday, and he rested in the shadow of this great god. A vision of sleep seized him at the hour (when) the sun was in the

Co-Regent Thutmose IV

Wikimedia Commons- Louvre Museum/ CC BY-SA

Tuthmosis IV
Menkheperure

zenith, and he found the majesty of this revered god speaking with his own mouth, as a father speaks with his son, saying: "Behold thou me! See thou me! my son Thutmose. I am thy father, Harmakhis-Khepri-Re-Atum, who will give to thee my kingdom on earth at the head of the living. Thou shalt wear the white crown and the red crown upon the throne of Keb, the hereditary prince. The land shall be thine in its length and breadth, that which the eye of the All-Lord shines upon. The food of the Two Lands shall be thine, the great tribute of all countries, the duration of a long period of years. My face is thine, my desire is toward thee. Thou shalt be to me a protector (for) my manner is as I were ailing in all my limbs ---. The sand of this desert upon which I am, has reached me; turn to me, to have that done which I have desired, knowing that thou art my son, my protector; come hither; behold, I am with thee, I am thy leader." When he had finished this speech, this king's-son awoke hearing this, he understood the words of this god, and he kept silent in his heart. He said: "Come, let us hasten to our house in the city; they shall protect the oblations for this god which we bring for him: oxen --- and all young vegetables; and we shall give praise [to] Wenn~fer,----Khaf[re], the statue made for Atum-Harmakhis---". (Breasted, p. 323 and 324.)

Left- The "Dream Stele" of Thutmose IV erected between the paws of the Great Sphinx in Giza. This stele is massive, as can be seen in the photos on the next page. This pharaoh did nothing in a small way. When he became emperor pharaoh, Amenhotep III, he made the most massive statues of any pharaoh and the largest number.

Randall Lee

Library of Congress/ Public domain
Old photo showing the Sphinx partially buried in sand and silt, much like during the time of Thutmose IV.

Mary Nell Lee
Dr. Ali Hassan, me and my late husband, Ron in front of the "Dream Stele." Measurements taken by Lepsius show it to be 7'2" wide and 11' 10" tall.

Thutmose IV's Obelisk
and Other Accomplishments

Following in the footsteps of his predecessors, Thutmose IV erected an obelisk. However, he took the easy route and completed one that had been begun by Thutmose III. It was the tallest of all the obelisks at 105 feet. Also, other obelisks were erected in pairs, unlike this one which was erected alone at Karnak.

The largest obelisk in the world, it was brought to Rome in 357 AD and placed in the Circus Maximus. It later collapsed and was rediscovered in 1587 in 3 separate pieces. It was then repaired and set up in the Piazza di San Giovanni in Rome where it remains today.

His accomplishments documented in his name of Thutmose IV are few. In his Konosso stele it relates that he participated in a military action in his 8th year to quell an uprising in Nubia, which seemed to happen regularly. Interestingly, he is accredited with establishing peaceful relations with the Mitanni then taking a Mitanni princess as a wife to seal the relationship. I suggest that this was accomplished by the emperor Amenhotep II and the offer of a Mittani wife was passed on to this co-regent since we have no records of his participating in any wars against the Mitanni as head of the army.

Wives and Mother

In the Luxor Temple depicting the birth of Amenhotep III (Thutmose IV when he becomes emperor) it shows his mother Mutemwiya giving birth to Amenhotep III. Therefore, scholars assigned her the position of being Thutmose IV's wife with the accepted belief that he was Amenhotep III's father instead of the same individual. As will be seen, everything falls into place once the data is looked at in a different light. I believe Mutemwiya was the mother of Thutmose IV and therefore was also the mother of Amenhotep III. Nowhere is Mutemwiya said to be Thutmose IV's wife.

Instead, two other women are depicted in his monuments and inscriptions as being his wives. Nefertari appears on numerous stelae as his wife. Another wife depicted is Iaret who is shown on a wall behind Thutmose IV as he is in the act of clubbing an enemy (see picture on page 143). Dated to year 7, Iaret was also his sister and is probably acting as his royal consort in conformity of the rules which require a royal "wife" of a pharaoh.

Thutmose IV and Tiaa, who is said to be his mother on this statue. I believe it is instead
Thutmose IV with his wife, Tiye, here spelled Tiaa.

Nefertari is known from depictions of her and Tiaa accompanying Thutmose IV. The official explanation is that Nefertari was his great wife and Tiaa was his mother. Yet nothing is known of Nefertari other than her presence on these stelae. In several of the stelae with Nefertari, a woman called Tiaa again appears. The official declaration is that she was his mother. Confusing, yes, but when Thutmose IV becomes the emperor, the evidence will make more sense. She was his favored wife, later spelled Tiye.

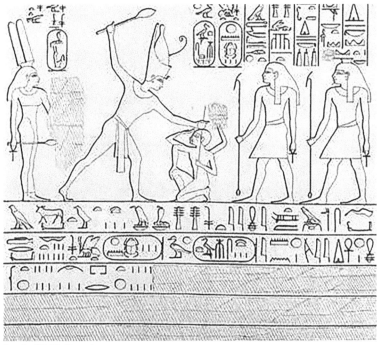

Lepsius/ Public Domain
Iaret with husband, Thutmose IV clubbing an enemy.

Recap of Who's Who in Chapter 11

Thutmose III was appointed to be the co-regent of Moses when he took the throne. When Moses fled, Thutmose III became the co-regent for Amenhotep I/Thutmose I, Moses' adopted grandfather.

When Amenhotep I/Thutmose I died, Thutmose III became the main emperor pharaoh and took the additional title of Amenhotep II. A co-regent was appointed for him and he was given the name Thutmose IV seen below. Both men were not of the royal family and came from Memphis.

Thutmose III

Amenhotep II

Thutmose IV

BC	Moses		Amen I	Thut I	Hat	Thut II	Thut III	Amen II	Thut IV
1507	19		20	8	2				
1506	20		21	9	3				
1505	21		22	10	4				
1504	22		23	11	5				
1503	23		24	12	6				
1502	24		25	13	7				
1501	25		26	14	8				
1500	26		27	15	9				
1499	27		28	16	10				
1498	28		29	17	11				
1497	29		30	18	12	1			
1496	30		31	19	13	2			
1495	31		32	20	14	3			
1494	32		33	21	15	4			
1493	33		34	22	16	5			
1492	34		35	23	17	6			
1491	35		36	24	18	7			
1490	36		37	25	19	8			
1489	37		38	26	20	9			
1488	38		39	27	21	10			
1487	39		40	28	22	11	22		
1486	40		41	29	23	12	23		
1485	41		42	30			24		
1484	42		43	31			25	1	1

Thutmose I/Amenhotep I celebrated his Sed Festival of 30 years of reign as Amenhotep I in 1497 BC. It was his 18th year as Thutmose I.

This was the year he promoted Senenmut (Moses) to Thutmose II. However, Moses remained in Thebes with his adopted grandfather and adopted mother, Hatshepsut. The emperor pharaoh did not move him and Hatshepsut (his regent) to Memphis to rule as he already had strong officials appointed there whom he trusted.

In Thutmose I's 28th year (40th year as Amenhotep I) the old pharaoh must have known he was getting near the time of his demise. He appointed Thutmose III as co-regent for Thutmose II (Moses) who one day was to become the emperor pharaoh when his adopted grandfather died.

Meanwhile, Thutmose II (Moses) fled in 1486 BC leaving a vacancy for the throne when Thutmose I/Amenhotep I died in 1484.

To resolve the empty throne issue, when Thutmose I died, Thutmose III was elevated to emperor pharaoh Amenhotep II and a co-regent, Thutmose IV, was appointed for him.

Chapter 12

THE EXODUS PHARAOH

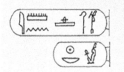

Amenhotep III
Nubmaatre

Thutmose IV Becomes Amenhotep III

Thutmose IV finally attained the title he had been long wanting, Amenhotep III. His first action as emperor pharaoh was the celebration of his Sed Festival in his year 1. This fact alone is evidence that he had been on the throne 30 years even though as co-regent.

Unlike the two previous emperor pharaohs, Thutmose IV favored his Amenhotep title as most of his recorded inscriptions are under that name, even accomplishments made during his co-regency when he was known as Thutmose IV.

Life was good for this emperor. The previous emperor, Thutmose III/ Amenhotep II, had secured the tribute from all the nations of the known world. The military was strong and had fortresses all throughout Canaan with the other nations subdued and made vassals of Egypt. Tribute poured in and the great wealth of the country continued to be beyond imagination.

 As I studied this king's reign, I was struck with the thought that this king was like the rich child raised wanting nothing and never having to work for anything. His extravagance was beyond imagination. He had more statues of himself than any other pharaoh. The country had been secured for him with vast amounts of tribute pouring in. No military actions of any real consequence were needed for all the surrounding nations viewed Egypt with great fear and respect.

All of these things made him the perfect picture of the pharaoh presented in the Bible as the one who refused to let God's people go. He was the head of the greatest nation known. His power was immense. He was possibly the richest king in the entire world. He possessed an immense force of slaves. The vassals of Egypt were secured by the previous pharaoh and there was no need for military intervention of any consequence.

It is my considered opinion that it is significant this pharaoh was on the throne at the time of the Exodus. His arrogance was exemplary. Other Egyptian kings until this time had participated in the building of the country. They had fought, they had worked, they appeared to consider the needs of the people. Little did he know what lay ahead. Because of his arrogance and great pride, he was doomed.

Birth and Wife

In his Luxor temple there is a depiction of his birth. Like Hatshepsut's royal birth depiction at Djeser-Djeseru, it shows Amenhotep III's mother,

Massive statue of Amenhotep III and his wife, Tiye, in the Cairo Museum.

Mutemwia, giving birth after being impregnated by Amun. She appears on the Colossi of Memnon with Amenhotep III and his wife Tiye and on the other walls and monuments which attest to his love for his mother.

Scholars state matter-of-factly that in his Luxor temple depiction of his birth, the god Amun comes in the form of Thutmose IV. But the name of his earthly father is not given in the inscription. This causes more confusion and is why it took so many years to get all the documentation I needed. Scholars will add the name of a person in an inscription that is not there.

The statue in the previous chapter shows Thutmose IV with a lady named Tiaa and she is said to be his mother. This conclusion was arrived at because of the belief that Thutmose IV and Amenhotep III are two different people. Instead I believe this statue is with his wife, Tiye, here spelled Tiaa.

Amenhotep III's wife Tiye was obviously the love of his life. The statues and representations of her with him show the great love and respect he had for her. He issued a series of commemorative scarabs, one which announces Tiye as his wife even though she was already his wife.

As emperor, he could proclaim a non-royal wife. This went against the system but just as Thutmose I used a novel means to elevate his daughter, Hatshepsut, to the position of royal heir, I believe Amenhotep III used the same principle by promoting a non-royal wife. The great prominence he gave her in all his statues and inscriptions show how deeply he loved her.

These scarabs also give the names of her parents, Yuya and Thuya whose tomb and mummies have been found. They appear foreign but it is not known where they are from.

Other scarabs tell of his great abilities as a hunter. One scarab issued in year 10 tells of his marriage to Gilukhepa, the daughter of the Mitanni king, Shuttarna. It tells of the 317 people who accompanied her which attests to Amenhotep III's great importance.

So far, at least 123 scarabs have been found which commemorate his lion hunts; 56 about his marriage to Tiye; 11 about a lake he was having dug for his wife; 5 about his bull hunts and 5 about the arrival of Gilukhepa. He left such an amazing amount of monuments and inscriptions that they fill many books. More statues of Amenhotep III have been identified than of any other pharaoh. More than 250 statues and likenesses have been found.

Amenhotep III took wives of daughters of the nations he dominated;

- Tadukhepa, the daughter of Mitanni ally Tushratta in year 36 counting his regnal years as co-regent,
- The daughter of the Babylonian king Kurigalzu,
- The daughter of the Babylonian king Kadashman-Enlil
- The daughter of the Arzawa king Tarhundaradu
- The daughter of the ruler of Ammia located in present day Syria.
- The final one was Gilukhepa, the daughter of Mitanni king Shuttarna in the tenth year of his reign as emperor which would be his last year.

He celebrated 3 Sed festivals, his first in his regnal year 1 as Amenhotep III,

Above- Statue head of Queen Tiye and one of the Marriage Scarabs declaring his marriage to the non-royal lady. This announcement was made in his regnal year 1 as the emperor. In fact, he was already married to her when he was co-regent.

which was his year 30 as Thutmose IV. This presents positive evidence that he ruled 30 years as co-regent before becoming the senior pharaoh in his 30th year.

Important Discovery in His Tomb

A discovery was made by a team from Waseda University who were working to restore the tomb of Amenhotep III. While working to conserve wall paintings, they discovered a figure of Amenhotep III standing next to Thutmose IV, both in equal position. This same type of picture was discussed in the last chapter concerning the Amada Temple of Amenhotep II with he and Thutmose III both depicted equally in the same scene.

This finding was unusual enough for attention to be brought to the find. Their conclusion was that they were co-regents. Instead, I propose that this proves that the two names are the same pharaoh. (KMT, Vol. 14, No. 4, Winter, p. 9.)

It is unheard of for a pharaoh to place another pharaoh on the wall of his tomb in an equal position. Especially Amenhotep III because he was not known as a generous person. I believe this is again solid evidence that he was one and the same person with both names.

Children

We don't know how many children he had because usually only female children were recorded. Four daughters are believed to be known- Sitamun, Henuttaneb, Iset and Nebetah. This practice was possibly because of how the royal line was supposed to pass through the daughter of the pharaoh. However, we know of at least two sons that he had and this is an issue that has been greatly misunderstood in my opinion.

Co-Regent Tutankhamun

When he became the emperor pharaoh, Amenhotep III appointed his eldest son, Tutankamun, to be his co-regent. This young son was only about 8 or 9 years old when he received the appointment. Needless to say, he was placed on the throne in name only. He had a vast number of officials who acted on his behalf, and they were all acting under the orders of his father.

At Meidum in the mortuary temple of the pyramid, there is a graffito. It is one of the two texts dated to year 1 from the reign of Amenhotep III:

Wikimedia Commons- ArchaiOptix/ CC BY-SA   *British Museum/ CC BY-SA*

Due to the very large amount of statues this king had made, we can view him through the years. In his very early statues, he looks almost like a teenager. As he grew older, his face filled out and took on a more mature appearance.

*"Year 30, under the person of the Dual King Nebmaatre, the son of Amen satisfied [with] truth, Amenhotep-heqawaset, lord of might, ruler of happiness, who loves him(?) who hates falsehood, **causing the male to sit down upon the seat of his father and establishing his inheritance [in] the land."***

The discovery of this graffito caused a great deal of discussion among the scholars. Some argued that it meant that this pharaoh was tired of the old way of appointing the co-regent through the royal wife. Perhaps that is true as Tut was the son of Tiye, his non-royal wife.

However, the argument among many was concerning the identity of this son of Amenhotep III. The concensus was that the son in the graffito was another son named Akhenaton. It is stated as fact by the scholars that Tutankhamun was not the son of this pharaoh but instead was his grandson. There is evidence of the identity of Tutankhamun's father which the scholars have chosen not to accept as factual. The Prudhoe or Soleb Lions, now in the British Museum, contain that evidence. Originally they sat guarding the Temple of Soleb in Nubia and contain an inscription by Tutankhamun:

"He who renewed the monument of (or 'for') his father, the King of Upper and Lower Egypt, Lord of the Two Lands, Nebmare, image of Re, Son of Re, Amenophis, Ruler of Thebes".

This firmly identifies Amenhotep III (Nebmare) as Tut's father. The very name, "Tutankhamun" comes from a word Amenhotep III used often:

"The word that Amenhotep III commonly used to describe the statues he ordered for his Theban temples is "tut". The root word means "to be like" and "to complete or perfect." ... At this point the statues might be referred to in the texts as "tut ankh," a living image (this being part of the name of Tutankhamun, "the living image of Amen") and could perform as the carefully devised deity that the statue expressed. However, the image as the receptacle of the divine essence needed to be recognizable both as the spirit residing within it and to the spirit living within it. The emphasis, therefore, on "perfected likeness" was considerable." ("Egypt's Dazzling Sun, Amenhotep III and His World," by Arielle P. Kozloff and Betsy M. Bryan with Lawrence M. Berman, p, 127.)

This connection with the word "tut" is just another evidence which points to him as being the father of Tutankamun. By including in his firstborn son's

Mary Nell Lee

The young boy, Tutankhamun, appointed co-regent as a 8 or 9 year old child. There aren't any statues of him as a very young boy. In the known statues, he looks to be from perhaps 12 or 13 years old through about 18 years old at the most. He died while still a teenage or perhaps 17- 19 years old.

name a word he used very often to stress the likeness of the pharaoh to the god was something very important to Amenhotep III.

More evidence which indicates Tutankhamun was the son of Amenhotep III are found in inscriptions in the Luxor temple. In the colonnade there, inscriptions ascribed to Tutankhamun refer to "his father, Nebmaatre" which is Amenhotep III.

This is not the accepted story of Tutankhamun. Different theories claim he is the son of Akhenaton who was actually his brother. Tutankhamun's mother was Tiye although recent reports have said he is the son of Akhenaton and one of his sisters. That conclusion by scholars will be explained in detail in the next chapter.

In my early years of research, I discovered how very confusing all the data appeared. But when I applied Ron's theory, I discovered how smoothly all the data fit into a cohesive pattern.

British Museum

One of the Soleb Lions which contains an inscription by Tutankhamun stating he made this for his father, Amenhotep III.

Tutankhamun was to be Amenhotep IV

Everything I found written about Amenhotep IV state as fact that this was Akhenaton. I propose instead that it was to be the name Tutankhamun would take when he became the emperor pharaoh. I propose any inscriptions which contain the name Amenhotep IV are referring to Tutankhamun.

The identification as Akhenton, his brother who would take the throne later, is based on the similarity of the statues of Amenhotep IV to later statues of Akhenaton. There is a strong family resemblance among their mother's family. It only makes sense that Tutankhamun and his younger brother, Akhenaton, would resemble each other.

A discovery was made recently and reported in 2013 which ties in with this identification. In the tomb of Vizier Amenhotep-Huy, the names of both Amenhotep III and Amenhotep IV were found on the same column. More importantly it dates to the beginning of the Sed Festival in the 30th year of Amenhotep III's reign counting his years as co-regent Thutmose IV. (KMT, vol. 25 no. 2 Summer 2014, pp 17- 27.) This was the year Amenhotep III became emperor and designated his son, Tutankhamun, as his co-regent.

Scholars state that this is proof of a co-regency between Amenhotep III and Amenhotep IV. I totally agree, except they identify Amenhotep IV as Akhenaton, instead of Tutankhamun.

Louvre Museum/ CC BY

Statue in the Louvre said to be Akhenaton but there is no name on the buckle. I propose it is instead Tutankhamen.

Wikimedia Commons- Einsamer Schütze / CC BY-SA

Wikimedia Commons- Marc Ryckaert/ CC BY-SA

Top- Statue of Tut from Hermopolis said to be Akhenaton.
Bottom-Tut at Karnak.

Oriental Institute- Daderot/ CC0

17 ft. statue of Tutankhamun from Medinet Habu that was usurped by two later pharaohs. It now bears the name of Horemheb and once bore the name Ay.

Recap of Who's Who in Chapter 12

Amenhotep III (also Thutmose IV)

Tutankhamun (also Amenhotep IV)

Thutmose IV became Amenhotep III when Thutmose III/Amenhotep II died. He appointed his eldest son, Tutankhamun as his co-regent. Statues of Tut were made with his future name of Amenhotep IV, however, he never lived to become the emperor pharaoh.

Snofru~commonswiki/ CC BY-SA

Tiye was the wife of Amenhotep III/ Thutmose IV and the mother of Tutankhamun.

Amenhotep III had at least one other son who later became pharaoh by the name of Akhenaton who will be discussed in a later chapter. He was the brother of Tutankhamun and their mother was Queen Tiye.

Ankhesenamun was depicted in young Tut's tomb as his wife. She was likely a full sister of Tutankhamun which would mean her father was Amenhotep III and her mother was Queen Tiye.

Chapter 13

BATTLE FOR THE FIRSTBORN

*Exo. 4:22 ... Thus saith the LORD, **Israel is my son, even my firstborn:***

Wikimedia Commons- Charles Foster/ Public Domain

The stage was set. Egypt basked in her luxury, most of it the product of the calloused hands of the Israelite slaves. When Moses was 80 years old in Midian, God spoke to him:

*Exo 4:19 And the LORD said unto Moses in Midian, Go, return into Egypt: for **all the men are dead which sought thy life.***

This is a crucial statement because it mentions "men", plural, who had sought Moses' life. His adopted grandfather would be one of those. The other would have been the man who was going to be his co-regent, Thutmose III. My timeline shows his adopted grandfather, Thutmose I, died just two years after Moses fled Egypt. Then Thutmose III/Amenhotep II died just 10 years before the Exodus when Moses was 71 years old. The present pharaoh Thutmose IV/ Amenhotep III was young when he was appointed and would not have known Moses.

Amenhotep III was the pharaoh of the Exodus. It was his year 39 and year 10 of young Tutankhamun when Moses returned to Egypt. God told Moses what to say to the pharaoh:

*Exo. 4:22 And thou shalt say unto Pharaoh, Thus saith the LORD, **Israel is my son, even my firstborn:** 23 And I say unto thee, Let my son go, that he may serve me: and if thou refuse to let him go, behold, **I will slay thy son, even thy firstborn.***

The first nine plagues completely devastated Egypt and were designed by God to prove the impotency of their multitude of gods. The God of Abraham wanted to show pharaoh that his magicians and his gods were helpless to the power of the great I Am.

It is beyond comprehension that the pharaoh would stubbornly refuse to let the people go after the devastation Egypt suffered. We can only understand this when Scripture tells us God hardened pharaoh's heart. It was necessary to God that the nation of Egypt be brought to their knees and know that He was the Lord.

The Origin of Passover

After the first nine plagues, God told Moses to tell the people of Israel that this would be the beginning of the first month of the year to them. He then instructed them on the 10th day of that month to take a lamb for each household without blemish, a male of the first year.

They were to keep the sweet little lamb with them until the 14th day of that same month, then kill it in the evening. After this they were to take the blood of the innocent little animal and strike it on the two side posts and the upper door post of the house in which they ate the lamb.

They were then to roast the lamb without breaking any of its bones and eat it with bitter herbs and unleavened bread. After this they were to be ready to leave, loins girded, shoes on and staff in hand.

Our understanding of this is of supreme importance. God was telling the people about the Blood of His Firstborn. By telling the people they were to commemorate this every year, He wanted to impress upon them the miraculous deliverance of the Israelites from Egypt.

But of greater importance, this was pointing forward to the final deliverance of all who accepted the Firstborn of God and His sacrifice as payment for their sins. Before the great multitude could be set free, they had to obey by placing the blood of the lamb on the lintel posts all around the door to the house. This required an act of faith and also obedience.

They were to separate completely from the Egyptians and gather in their own homes. We know that a mixed multitude left with the Israelites so apparently if any of them begged to come into the house of the Israelites, the blood covered them as well. The sacrificial lamb represented the Lamb of God, the future Messiah.

The events of the Exodus from Egypt were laying the foundation for preparing God's chosen people to take the knowledge of Him to the world. It was an event like none other in the history of the world. It was of such importance to God that He miraculously preserved evidence which has not been acknowledged by the secular world.

Before the 10th plague God told Moses to:

Exo 11:2 Speak now in the ears of the people, and let every man borrow of his neighbour, and every woman of her neighbour, jewels of silver, and jewels of gold…. 12:35 And the children of Israel did according to the word of Moses; and they borrowed of the Egyptians jewels of silver, and jewels of gold, and raiment: 36 And the LORD gave the people favour in the sight of the Egyptians, so that they lent unto them such things as they required. And they spoiled the Egyptians.

The Hebrew words in this text that are translated "borrow" and "lent" are the same Hebrew word, "shaal." This word simply means "ask," "demand," "request," "give," etc. Only six times in the entire Bible is it translated "borrow" and two times as "lend" or "lent." But 87 times it is translated "ask" and in excess of 60 times is it translated to read other words which mean simply "ask".

These verses are stating that they "asked" for these things, as God had told them to do so they would not be a destitute nation. And the Egyptians complied with whatever they asked. The fear of God was in the Egyptians after the terrible plagues which had befallen them by the Hand of the Israelites' God.

It is difficult for us to imagine such events as the plagues. But as the evidence unfolds, all indications point to a complete devastation of ancient Egypt at that time, consistent with the first nine plagues. Then came the final plague:

Exo 12:29 And it came to pass, that at midnight the LORD smote all the firstborn in the land of Egypt, from the firstborn of Pharaoh that sat on his throne unto the firstborn of the captive that was in the dungeon; and all the firstborn of cattle. 30 And Pharaoh rose up in the night, he, and all his servants, and all the Egyptians; and there was a great cry in Egypt; for there was not a house where there was not one dead. 31 And he called for Moses and Aaron by night, and said, Rise up, and get you forth from among my people, both ye and the children of Israel; and go, serve the LORD, as ye have said. 32 Also take your flocks and your herds, as ye have said, and be gone; and bless me also.

The Death of Pharaoh's Firstborn Son

The firstborn son of Amenhotep III, Tutankhamun, went to bed that night like any other. In the quiet of the night as the cool breeze of evening wafted through the palace, the young man was struck by the unseen angel of God and died.

His father, Amenhotep III, was not a firstborn son and he lived to see the Hand of God bring him to his knees. Had official protocol been followed and the firstborn son of the last pharaoh been the pharaoh at the time of the Exodus, he would have also died.

God miraculously preserved the evidence of young Tutankhamun for the ages. Even though the young co-regent never truly reigned as a pharaoh, the contents of his tomb captured the attention of the world in the 1920's right up until today.

The heartbreak of the pharaoh cannot be fathomed. The entire nation was full of the cries of mourning for the loss of their family members. Finally, the pharaoh had been defeated and he told Moses to take his people and go, and bless him.

When the children of Israel left Egypt, they were to go a three day journey into the desert to worship God then return. But instead they kept going according to God's instructions.

They continued their journey away from Egypt. The Egyptians most certainly had messengers posted all across the Sinai Peninsula and they were

Both images on this page– Google Earth
The general path of the journey of the Israelites.

Wadi Watir, the narrow passage God led the great multitude into as they traveled to the Red Sea crossing. The huge beach at Nuweiba was their destination.
Exo. 14:3   For Pharaoh will say of the children of Israel, They are entangled in the land, the wilderness hath shut them in.

Mary Nell Lee

Ron near the exit of Wadi Watir onto the beach of Nuweiba. The wadi twists and turns the entire way, making it seem like the passage is ending.

capable of signaling with mirrors to relay that they had escaped.

Moses, by the command of God, was leading the people to the mountain God had chosen, Mount Sinai where Moses had first encountered the burning bush. But when they reached the northward turn Moses had taken to go to Midian, God told him to stop and turn and go a different way.

When the multitude turned to the south, they entered into a narrow, winding wadi. At times this snaking, narrow canyon is at most about 75 feet wide, looking always as if it were coming to a dead end just up ahead. Traveling through this narrow passage would have been terrifying, not being able to see what lay up ahead. The approximately 18 mile journey would have put even the bravest to the test.

When Pharaoh heard that they had fled, his anger must have been unimaginable. By this time, his great sorrow had turned to blinding fury. He assembled his entire army- 600 chosen chariots, and all the chariots of Egypt and captains over every one, and in fierce anger, pursued the great multitude to the Red Sea, the Gulf of Aqaba.

The divisions of the army were named after the gods and when the army set out to war, elaborate ceremonies were performed at the various temples asking the various gods to give them victory over their foes. All military victories were directly attributed to the favor of the gods. Sometimes the priests would accompany the army to the battlefield in hopes that the gods would show special favor in their battles.

The evidence in the ancient records indicate that when Pharaoh and his army set out after Moses and the great multitude, he took with him the entire priesthood of all the gods of Egypt. He had seen the power of the true God. If the Egyptian army ever needed supernatural intervention by the hands of their gods, it was at this time.

The great multitude finally exited the winding wadi and found themselves on a large beach, more than large enough to contain all the people and their flocks and herds. But to the right, the mountains met the sea and there was no possible way to travel in that direction, while to the left the mountains encroached on the water and the available beach was far too narrow to pass. The people had no idea where to turn.

The complaints of the people were hurled at Moses. Even after the miracles the people had seen, their faith was wavering. Moses tried to tell them to wait on the Lord for He would deliver them.

But the Egyptian army, led by the pharaoh, appeared exiting the wadi. Fear filled the hearts of the multitude. Deliverance seemed impossible. Then Moses told them, *"the Egyptians whom you have seen today, ye shall see them again no more for ever. The Lord shall fight for you, and ye shall hold your peace."*

Suddenly, the pillar of fire which had been in front of the multitude rose up and settled behind them, between them and the Egyptians. It became darkness to the Egyptians and a great light to the children of Israel. Moses then stretched out his hand over the sea and it parted. The great multitude then crossed the great distance of about ten miles on dry land. Pharaoh's army pursued them and angels removed the chariot wheels and the army became greatly afraid and tried to backtrack to the shore. But it was too late.

On the opposite shore, Moses stretched out his hand over the sea and the waters crashed together, drowning the entire army. This was a Divine miracle beyond the comprehension of man. God had long ago prepared the large beach, the winding wadi, and the pathway through the waters which, although very deep, was gently sloping and provided a viable path for the people, their wagons and their flocks. Only the Creator of all things could have done such a work. And it was the last thing the Egyptians in the great army saw.

In the morning, the children of Israel saw the dead bodies of the Egyptians lying on the shore. The soldiers on chariots had their weapons fastened on their bodies and the people gathered the weapons. They were now free from their great enemy and they were now armed as they continued their journey to Mount Sinai.

The watchmen all through the mountains and along the desert path back to Egypt signaled word of the calamity. When this message arrived back at the palace in Memphis, it was too fantastic to be believed- the entire army, all of the priesthood, and the pharaoh himself had drowned in the Red Sea. The confusion, grief, and agony of the entire country is impossible to comprehend. It became utmost in the minds of those remaining in Egypt that all knowledge of what had happened must be kept secret or else they would fall prey to their enemies.

There was another immediate need. Throughout the entire land, every family had to arrange for the burial of their first-born stricken by the angel of death, but there was no priesthood to administer the rites.

Tutankhamun's Burial

About 3,300 years later, another miracle would be revealed. In 1906, Theodore Davis was excavating in the Valley of the Kings where many royal tombs had been found. He found a blue pitcher with the little known name Tutankhamun on it in a cache.

The next year he found a tunnel and followed it to a room 21 feet underground. In this room was a broken wooden casket containing several leaves of gold with silhouettes of Tutankhamun, his wife Ankhesenamun and Ay, the "Divine Father."

Metropolitan Museum of Art/ CC0
Linen from the cache Theodore Davis found. They assumed at first they had found the burial of the young Tutankhamun.

In a well-shaft about a hundred yards to the south of this, they found other objects, some being pots with stoppers bearing the name of Tutankhamun. One pot was wrapped in a piece of cloth dated regnal year 6 of Tutankhamun. Small bags whose contents had turned to dust were found next to a heap of linen for wrapping a mummy. Included in the cloth were three semicircular wig covers of sorts and 50 mummification bandages specially woven with selvages for that same purpose.

The assumption by the excavators was they had found the remains of the burial of young Tutankhamun.

Metropolitan Museum of Art/ CC0

A floral collar from Tutankhamun's cache.

They found some floral necklaces of cornflowers and blue lotuses interlaced upon a ground of olive leaves with blue beads which they assumed guests had worn at his service. They thought they had found his tomb and that it had been ravaged by robbers. But it was not his tomb.

In 1922, when Howard Carter was continuing to search for royal tombs in the area, he found the actual tomb of this relatively unknown young king. Without a doubt, it was the most spectacular discovery the world had ever seen! Books speak of the mysteries surrounding the young Tut but these mysteries can only be properly understood in the context of the Scriptures.

The greatest treasures ever found in a royal tomb were in this tomb for a minor figure of history and all the scholars agree that the tomb was not constructed for a king. Royal burials of the pharaohs were extravagant but Tutankhamun's tomb was anything but that.

The earlier discovery of the cache with items containing Tutankhamun's name indicated something very strange. The implication was the mummification process and was likely done at the cache site instead of the embalming shop.

These photos all show the tomb of Tut in its original condition.

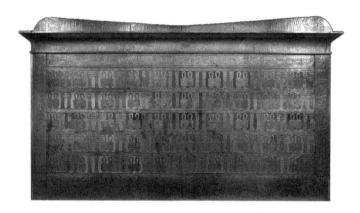

Wikimedia Commons- Je-str/ CC BY-SA

Left- Within the tomb was a large golden shrine, 10'10" by 16'5" by 9' seen in the top image. Within this shrine were 3 more shrines, one within the other. Within the smallest shrine was a red sandstone sarcophagus of magnificent work which had a broken lid of rough granite that had been hastily painted to match the sarcophagus.

Wikimedia Commons- A. Parrot/ CC BY-SA

Above- middle coffin.   **Below**- innermost coffin which is 2,448 lbs. of 22 kt. gold.

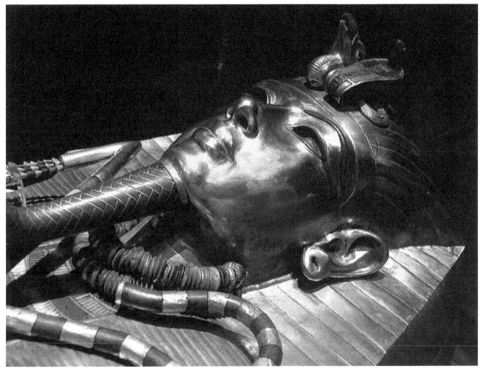

Jon Bodsworth/ Copyrighted Free Use

Usually for a royal mummy and funeral, 70 days were required for the process then the body was carefully wrapped and placed in the coffin. A procession was then made to the tomb. But his tomb and the evidences in the earlier cache location left the impression of haste.

When the tomb was first opened, everything was in disorder. Chariots had been taken apart and never reassembled. It presented a picture of chaos. It clearly had been done in a great rush. The exquisite items would normally have been set up in proper order with the chariots put together.

The first reaction of all who saw it was shock and awe. The clear implication was that the funeral items had been loaded into the tomb in great haste. No other major tomb displayed this sort of disarray. Some claimed the tomb had been robbed which is why there was such a confusion of items. However, there is no evidence it was ever robbed.

Within the tomb was a large, golden shrine, 10'10" by 16'5" by 9'. Within this shrine were three more shrines, one within the other. Within the smallest shrine was a red sandstone sarcophagus of magnificent work which had a

Wikimedia Commons-Exclusive to the Times/Copyrighted Free Use

Howard Carter looking into the second coffin at the third and last interior coffin. The interior coffin is 2,448 pounds of pure 22 kt. gold.

broken lid of rough granite that had been hastily painted to match the sarcophagus. See the composite photo on page 170.

The funeral mask on young Tutankhamun when the middle coffin was first opened.

Pixabay

Gold mummy mask found on Tutankhamun.

Inside this sarcophagus was a gold covered wooden mummiform. The feet of the mummiform were too long to fit in the sarcophagus so they simply planed the feet and left the wood shavings where they fell beneath it.

Within this mummiform coffin were two more, one within the other. The last one that contained the mummy of Tutankhamun was 2,448 pounds of pure 22 kt. gold. Inside was the mummy wearing a solid gold death mask.

Randall Lee

A statue of Amenhotep III when he was quite young. The mummiforms and the mask were made in his images as he progressively aged.

It didn't make sense. To add to the mystery, the names on a vast number of objects in the tomb had been altered and changed from another name to that of Tutankhamun.

In addition, with the multitude of items in the tomb, there was no crown of any sort anywhere. The treasures in the tomb were beyond comprehension.

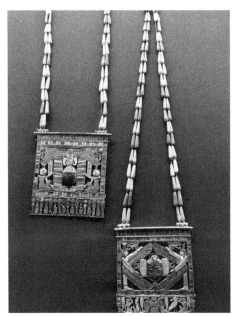

Necklaces from Tutankhamun's tomb. The one of the right matches one on the wall of Kheruef's tomb that was given to Amenhotep III.

The workmanship was superb yet the sarcophagus had a makeshift lid. The tomb itself was clearly not built for a king.

The condition of the mummy was a great shock as well. The usual mummification process involved immersing the body in natron for 70 days to remove all moisture from the body. However when Tutankhamun's coffin was opened, his mummy was in very poor condition because this procedure had not been done properly.

All the soft tissue of his mummy was carbonized by a sort of spontaneous combustion of the unguents poured on the body which was brought about by the heat and humidity in the sealed coffin. This humidity would not have been there if his body had undergone the complete mummification process.

It appears with all the firstborns to bury and no priests to perform the elaborate ceremonies, the bodies were quickly embalmed, wrapped and then buried in haste.

A positive indication of the time of his death comes from the flowers buried with him. The mandrakes and cornflowers reached maturity in late March and April placing the time of his death at the exact time of the Passover.

Most likely no tomb had been started for the young boy and no one knows for whom this tomb was made. But it is known that many items in the tomb were not made for him. Also in his tomb were two mummified fetuses, probably his children that never made it to full term or perhaps the fetuses of other family members who lost a first-born son to the 10th plague.

The evidence shows that the funeral equipment made at great expense for his father, Amenhotep III, was used to bury his son. Amenhotep III did not need them as he never returned from his last fateful military excursion to the Red Sea.

In addition to the names on many objects being altered, the faces on the coffins are not the face of young Tutankhamun but are the face of his father as a young man and then as an adult. Many statues of a younger Amenhotep III are very similar to the death mask and mummiforms found with the young Tutankhamun.

Concerning the fabulous articles of jewelry found there, in the tomb of Kheruef, an artisan under Amenhotep III, is a picture of tomb owner Kheruef presenting Pharaoh Amenhotep III with magnificent jewelry he had made. Many scholars have noticed that these are virtually identical with items found in Tutankhamun's tomb. Another proof that the items belonged to his father.

But there were other items in the tomb which led to such confusion that it caused a completely different belief in who young Tutankhamun really was. Those things, however, were not placed in his tomb at his initial burial. It would be opened again at a later date. That will be explained as events unfold.

For now, Egypt was in mourning and the children of Israel were traveling through the wilderness to Mount Sinai.

Randall Lee
Amenhotep III, the pharaoh of the Exodus who drowned in the Red Sea while pursuing the Israelites.

Chapter 14

Protect the Nation

Upon the death of the pharaoh and the loss of the priesthood and the army, Egypt was in much the same state as our country would be if we had lost our President, Vice-President, all the Secretaries of the various offices, as well as the Senate and House of Representatives. But they had one advantage we wouldn't have- they were extremely isolated and communication was such that they were able to keep their situation secret and it was vital that the secret not get out.

The palaces in the two capitals, Memphis and Thebes, were still standing. The country itself displayed the devastation Egypt had suffered during the plagues but the country was still standing.

After burying all their dead, the next thing they needed was a new king. Traditionally a new pharaoh was the first born son of the reigning king by the royal wife. But these were not normal times. There was not a single first born son in all of Egypt among man or beast.

Even if they appointed a new king, they had no army except for the troops stationed in Canaan, Syria and Lebanon in the fortresses overseeing and protecting their vassals. While there are no records in the ancient documents of Egypt telling of the events right after the Exodus, there was a very important stone cuneiform document found in Turkey.

Hittite Document of Mursili

In the ancient Hittite archives at Hattusa, today called Bogazkoy, there was found an inscription left behind by Mursili, the son of the Hittite king Suppiluliuma who was on the throne at the time of the death of the pharaoh. It told a strange tale.

The Hittite king Suppiluliuma had been in Carchemish and sent some of his troops to Amqa located in Lebanon, to attack the Egyptian stronghold:

"While my father was down in the country of Karkamis, he dispatched Lupakkis and Tessub-zalmas to the country of Amqa. They proceeded to attack the country of Amqa and brought deportees, cattle (and) sheep home before my father." ("Ancient Near Eastern Texts," edited by James B. Pritchard, p. 319)

Wikimedia Commons– Koppas/ CC BY-SA

Hittite relief in the Museum of Anatolian Civilizations in Ankara, Turkey.

He then relates a very puzzling letter his father received from Egypt:

"When the people of the land of Egypt heard about the attack on Amqa, they became frightened. Because, to make matters worse, their lord Bibhururiyas had just died, the Egyptian queen who had become a widow, sent an envoy to my father and wrote him as follows: 'My husband died and I have no son. People say that you have many sons. If you were to send me one of your sons, he might become my husband. I am loath to take a servant of mine and make him my husband." (Pritchard, p. 319.)

This request by the widowed queen was unheard of in all of ancient Egypt both before and after this. It was likely a decision made out of desperation. After all, the Hittite nation was the upcoming threat to Egypt's dominance of the region.

Amenhotep III had maintained good relations with the Mitanni through royal marriages with Mitanni princesses. But this was a totally different situation. The Hittites were powerful and a real threat to Egypt if they learned the truth. The widowed queen offered to take a Hittite son and make him the king of Egypt. This was simply unheard of. Suppiluliuma was obviously stunned by the request.

This widowed queen made it clear that all left in her country were her servants. I imagine those left alive in Egypt, including the wives of the deceased Amenhotep III and Tutankhamun, were at a complete loss as to what to do.

And we don't know for sure which wife wrote the letter. Scholars assign the name of the dead pharaoh "Bibhuria" as "Tutankhamun," for one of his names was "Neb-kheper-ru-re," however, it could be transliterated "Neb-maat-Re," which was one of the names of Amenhotep III. Either way, the evidence is equally strong. Whoever sent the letter, the evidence is clear that a catastrophe had taken place in Egypt.

So bizarre was this request that at first Suppiluliuma didn't believe her, as his son continues:

"When my father heard that, he called the great into council (saying): 'Since of old such a thing has never happened before me'. He proceeded to dispatch Hattu-zitis, the chamberlain, (saying): 'Go! Bring you reliable information back to me. They may try to deceive me: As to whether perhaps they have a prince bring reliable information back to me!' During Hattu-zitis' absence in the land of Egypt my father vanquished the city of Karkamis… The Egyptian envoy, the Honorable Hanis, came to him. Because my father had instructed Hattu-zitis while sending him to the land of Egypt as follows: 'Perhaps they have a prince; they may try to deceive me and do not really want one of my sons to (take over) the kingship,' the Egyptian queen answered my father in a letter as follows: 'Why do you say: 'They may try to deceive me'? If I had a son, would I write to a foreign country in a manner which is humiliating to myself and to my country? You do not trust me and tell me even such a thing. He who was my husband died and I have no sons. Shall I perhaps take one of my servants and make him my husband? I have not written to any other country, I have written (only) to you. People say that you have many sons. Give me one of your sons and he is my husband and king in the land of Egypt.' Because my father was generous, he complied with the lady's wishes and decided for (sending) the son." (Pritchard, p. 319).

Queen Tiye, the great love of Amenhotep III. She was the mother of Tutankhamun and had numerous other children.

Suppiluliuma finally believed her and sent a son. However, that son never made it to Egypt as the account continues:

"My father sent foot soldiers and charioteers who attacked the country of Amka, Egyptian territory. Again he sent troops, and again they attacked it. When the Egyptians became frightened, they asked outright for one of his sons to (take over) the kingship. But when my father gave them one of his sons, they killed him as they led him there." (Pritchard, p. 395).

This presents a picture of a frightened nation attempting to save itself. The powerful Hittites were now their greatest fear. The only army Egypt had left were the troops stationed in their vassal territories and they would soon need to be recalled. The population of men in the country was greatly reduced except for the lowly class that the pharaoh's wife called her servants.

Time slowly passed and the Egyptians tried to pick up the pieces and go on with their lives but it was difficult. The only thing they had in their favor was the fact that the country was situated in a manner that they were isolated from the rest of the world. No one could enter the country without being detected far before they arrived. Careful precautions were taken to see that the true situation was not discerned by others.

The only people who possessed any authority to do anything within the government were the members of the deceased Amenhotep III's family, especially his wife, Tiye. Queen Tiye was known by all to be greatly loved and respected by her deceased husband and she wielded great power simply by being his widow.

She was the first queen to have her name written on many official announcements made by the pharaoh, one example being his marriage to a foreign princess. Her name was even enclosed in a cartouche which was reserved for the true royals. We don't have a lot of information about this lady's background but we do know who her parents were because the pharaoh put their names on scarabs dedicated to his marriage to his wife.

Yuya and Thuya were the names of her parents. Their tomb was found in 1905 and contained objects and coffins on the order of a royal burial. They had titles within Amenhotep III's court. They also had a son named Anen who was a second prophet of Amun but evidence points to his having died before Amenhotep became the emperor pharaoh. Though it is not stated anywhere, evidence indicates that Ay was another son of Yuya and Thuya and therefore he was the brother of Amenhotep III's wife, Tiye. He was vizier for Tutankhamun, the highest position in the cabinet.

On the wall in Tut's tomb, Ay (on the right) is administering the rites for his burial.

Pharaoh Ay- a Placeholder

Time passed in the devastated Egypt. A new pharaoh appeared on the throne. We don't know how long after the Exodus this occured but most likely it was relatively soon, possibly within the year. Ay, the brother of Tiye, was chosen to fill the void. The brother-in-law of Amenhotep III needed justification to the throne and apparently he associated Anhkesenamun, the widow of young Tutankhamun as his queen.

I'm not sure how young Ankhesenamun felt about being symbolically married to a much older man, but I'm sure everyone did what they felt was best for

Wikimedia Commons- Miguel Hermoso Cuesta / CC BY-SA

Pharaoh Ay. This is believed to represent him although there is no name on the statue head. It was found in the studio of an artist who worked for the royal family a few years after his reign.

the country. However, the only evidence of Anhkesenamun as his queen was a scarab with both royal names on it incorporated on a ring.

On the wall of the young Tutankhamun's tiny, jumbled tomb, it is Ay who is shown administering his funeral rights. He does not appear as a pharaoh but instead as "the divine father," a high priest dressed in leopard skin. Ay had been vizier for young Tutankhamun and was probably given this office due to his relation to Amenhotep III's wife, Tiye. I suggest that Ay was close to the young co-regent for whom he was chief official because he was also his uncle.

It was a necessary move to appoint the elder Ay to the throne and he was just a placeholder until another young son of Amenhotep III's became old enough to take the throne. This younger son and brother to Tutankhamun was obviously too young to take the throne right after his father and brother's death. With Ay on the throne, Tiye could maintain her hold on the future royal office for her young son.

In later inscriptions, Ay is shown with a wife named Tey. I believe she is the same Tiye who is his sister and the wife of the drowned Amenhotep III. He most likely named her as his royal consort to firm up his position as pharaoh. Or more likely, Tiye made the arrangement as I believe she wielded the power. This is a common practice, the marriage of brothers and sisters among the royal families. It is also the accepted and traditional method of passing the lineage of pharaohs.

There is little other evidence of Ay's reign and his reign is estimated at around 4 years although some scholars believe it may have been as long as 14 years. With so little documentation available, it could have lasted a few years longer than that in order for Tutanhkamun's younger brother to attain a reasonable age to take the throne. The argument for an extended period of time is the fact that when this young man attained the throne, he already had a wife and children.

"I Am Entirely Innocent!"

There is one interesting fact concerning Ay relating to the incident of Hittite king Suppiluliuma's son being killed when he was sent to Egypt to be the husband of the widowed pharaoh's wife. A letter discovered in the Hittite archives from Ay tells of his denial of the charges of having the king's son killed. This clearly proves the Hittite king had accused him of this heinous crime.

"Your accusations have no justification ... You are simply spoiling for a fight against me .. .I seek peace and brotherhood with you. As for your son's death of that I am entirely innocent!" (Letters of the Great Kings, by Trevor Bryce, p. 188.)

The truth will probably never be known concerning what happened to the young Hittite prince.

Chapter 15

DETERIORATION OF EGYPT

In time, the younger son of Amenhotep III by his wife Tiye came of age and was promoted as the new pharaoh. His name was Akhenaton. After studying records for years concerning this young man, I found only confusion. I will just present the basic facts I believe are pertinent.

Akhenaton and his wife, Nefertiti with some of their children.

Randall Lee
Pharaoh Akhenaton, the brother of Tutankhamun.

Akhenaton became the pharaoh when he was a young man. We have no idea how old he was when he came to the throne but he appears with a wife and children.

The indication is that this son was quite young at the time of the death of his father, Amenhotep III. It was more than four years before he attained adulthood and for this reason it is possible that Ay reigned longer than four years as they waited for the young man to attain enough years to rule.

His mother, Tiye was still alive and, I believe, very much in control. This young man, I reiterate, is believed by scholars to have been first called Amenhotep IV at the beginning of his reign but I reject that conclusion.

Inscriptions containing a cartouche of Amenhotep IV were actually referring to Tutankhamun during his lifetime. Prior to his death, that would have been the title he would have assumed when he became the emperor. Statues were often made in advance to someone taking the main throne. In the case of young Tut, he never made it to the senior pharaoh position.

Loss of Slave Labor

When Akhenaton ascended the throne, a new city called Akhetaten (also known as Amarna) was built to be the new capital, located relatively centered between Memphis and Thebes. Strangely, the city was built mostly of dried mud brick which scholars think was to speed up the operation. Instead, I believe it is a reflection of the fact that Egypt had lost its entire slave population, the children of Israel, who had done the work prior to this. Egypt simply did not have the labor force needed for massive cut stone construction.

The artwork changed drastically. There is no known reason for this. Depictions of people with oddly shaped heads and protruding bellies were some of the hallmarks of this new style.

However, not all of the art was this distorted. One of the most beautiful pieces of Egyptian art is the bust of Akhenaton's wife, Nefertiti.

Wikimedia Commons- Pichard Mortel/ CC BY

Bizarre depiction of Akhenaton from a wall in Amarna. Most of his art is of this style but not all.

Wikimedia Commons- Philip Pikart / CC BY-SA

Bust of Akhenaton's wife, Nefertiti, in the Berlin Museum.

This is a more realistic depiction of how Akhenaton really must have looked.

Wikimedia Commons- Jean-Pierre Dalbéra from Paris, France / CC BY
More realistic statue heads of Akhenaton's wife, Nefertiti and Akhenaton.

The studio of a sculptor in Amarna was found with a number of statues that appeared more realistic. The statue heads there depict Akhenaton more as a mature man. This indicates more time went by.

During Akhenaton's reign, the previous pharaoh, Ay, was given the royal titles "Fan bearer on the right of the King," "Acting Scribe of the King," "God's Father," "Master of All the Horses of his Majesty," and "Chief of Archers." His father, Yuya, held the position of "Master of the Horse" under the deceased Amenhotep III, as well as "prophet of Min" and "Superintendent of the Cattle." To the best of my knowledge, this is the only known time a pharaoh left office while alive and served under another pharaoh. Normally, a pharaoh was king for life. This practice has to do with their religious beliefs that the king is the earthly embodiment of the god. But religious beliefs were about to change.

Abandoning the Old Gods

The thing Akhenaton is most known for is his promotion of a new religion. This is major evidence of what had occurred in Egypt.

At the time of the Exodus, all the gods of Egypt had let the nation down drastically. Almost the entire (if not the entire) priesthood had drowned along with the army. Only the older, retired men were left of the upper class of the government. It was the perfect setting for a new religious system to be established. No one had faith in the old gods any longer.

This new religion was not something the young Akhenaton devised. It most certainly was his mother and his uncle, Ay, who advised this approach to a new form of worship.

Atenism was the name of this new religion; however, the god Aten was not new. Aten was a minor form of the sun-god. But the difference in this new official religion was the almost complete abandonment of all the other gods, especially Amun who was the god of his father. This presents a vivid picture of a nation who had lost faith in their gods and goddesses.

Wikimedia Commons- Einsamer Schütze / CC BY-SA

The city of Amarna was built of mud bricks. Today little remains are intact.

There were no statues except those of the royal family as all others were viewed as idolatry. The sun was worshiped in open air temples. Only pictures of Pharaoh Akhenaton and his family were on the walls everywhere.

It was a religion for the royal family and no real accommodations were made for the people to participate. Akhenaton was considered the prophet and perhaps the incarnation of the Aten. The propaganda promoted was that Aten would take care of everyone through Akhenaton's prayers.

But Aten was not a completely unknown god to the Egyptians. He began to appear in the reign of Akhenaton's father, Thutmose IV/Amenhotep III. As Thutmose IV, he had issued scarabs which featured Aten as a god of war. One of his names as the senior pharaoh Amenhotep III was Tjekhen-Aten which meant "radiance of Aten." He had slowly begun promoting the cult of Aten, only not exclusively. I believe it was most likely his wife, Tiye, who was the adherent to Aten and he was trying to please her.

New Royal City of Amarna

At the new city, Amarna, there were several buildings that were associated with Amenhotep III. For this reason, scholars have made the claim that Amenhotep III was alive during the time of Akhenaton but this is just more of the confusion:

"... The fact that several buildings at Amarna were associated with Amenophis III only serves to emphasise the importance there of the cult of dead ancestors, since houses of Thutmosis I, Amenophis II and Thutmose IV are also mentioned at Amarna, and no one would claim that those kings ever lived there." ("Akhenaton, King of Egypt," by Cyril Aldred, p. 174.)

The family of Akhenaton wanted to stress their relationship with the old pharaoh who had died in the Red Sea. It was their connection to the throne.

Tomb of Tutankhamun Reopened

The ancient Egyptians had many beliefs about the afterlife which were strictly observed. One belief was their kings were the earthly embodiment of the gods yet were still human. Their complicated beliefs, especially concerning the afterlife, required that the royal family and close officials make ample provisions for their ancestors in their tombs. To fail to do so could result in dire consequences for those at fault.

For this reason, several years after the rapid mummification and burial of young Tutankhamun, his tomb was again opened by the royal family of Amarna. New items were placed into his tomb which reflected the name of the god Aten. During their lifetimes, the main god of Tutankhamun and Amenhotep III was the god Amun which is obvious in the hieroglyphs in almost all the objects in the tomb. But after the great catastrophe of the Exodus, Amun fell from favor, as did all the other gods because of their failure to protect Egypt from the power of the God of Israel.

Cartouches on objects placed in his tomb by the Amarna family showed his name as Tutank-aten, reflecting the name of Aten. To prove that these items were placed in the tomb after the original burial, it is evidenced in the notes of when the tomb was first found and opened. In 1922, Carter found in the entrance to this tomb a piece of a box with the name of Akhenaton, his wife and Meryetaten, their daughter. This indicates that a number of years had gone by since the original burial. Perhaps as much as ten or more years since Akhenaton was married and had a daughter.

This shows how strongly they believed in the power of the dead. Those who buried Tutankhamun were taking no chances- they insured that young Tutankhamun would be accepted by Aten. They were also ensuring their own afterlife would be provided for. If Aten turned out to be the true god, this proved their loyalty.

The records on the walls of the public buildings were meant for the public to see but the items in the tomb were never meant for mortal eyes, only the eyes of the gods and the deceased. They had summoned a new god because they were desperate after the failure of the old gods. This was not propaganda. The people were never supposed to see inside that tomb.

I believe it was this very discovery that caused the early archaeologists and scholars to believe that Tutankhamun's reign came after his brother Akhenaton's reign instead of years before. The items with his name changed to include "Aten" in them caused great confusion.

There is also mention of someone by the name of Smenkhkare in the ancient records who is an unknown person. Since he is mentioned and since there are so many theories concerning who he was, I will present mine. Since his name is mentioned on a ring found in Amenhotep III's compound at Malqata, I am of the opinion that he is Tutankhamun's younger brother who became Akhenaton. If not, perhaps he is another younger brother. But I have not devoted a great deal of study on the subject since there is such a dearth of information available.

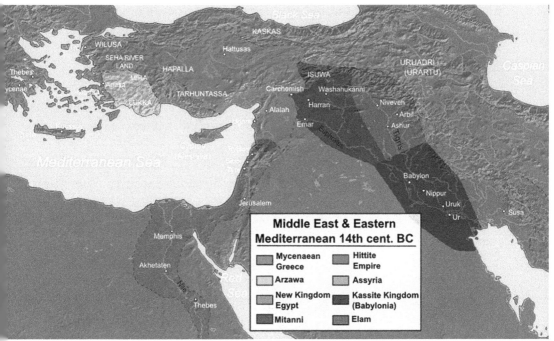

The kingdoms during the time of Egypt's domination. The kingdom of Amurru, under Egypt's dominion, is shown in magenta just below the purple/blue of the Hittite kingdom.

It had now been a number of years since the Exodus, perhaps 15 or even as much as 25 years, and the country must have struggled tremendously. The lower cast as well as the remaining royals had given up on the gods. The new king was nothing like the pharaohs of the past. Akhenaton and his family stayed at his palace in Amarna and had no interaction with the people.

The Amarna Letters Revealed Chaos

We have no idea how long it took to organize a new army and a new government. But we do have some idea of what was happening outside of Egypt with their vassals and other nations. I do not accept that it was a random discovery which revealed this picture of the chaos that ensued. I believe this discovery of the Amarna Letters was Divinely arranged.

This most exciting discovery made at the city of Amarna was a cache of 382 clay tablets representing official communications between the pharaohs of the time right after the Exodus and the kings of other nations and rulers of cities and small kingdoms in Canaan and Syria who were vassal states. Found in 1887, These letters offer solid proof that writing was not only extremely well developed by this time, but that Egypt communicated with the foreign powers in Akkadian. Not only did Egypt possess their hieroglyphics, demotic and hieratic writing but also cuneiform. These letters are referred to by EA and the number assigned to them by the translators.

There were several letters addressed to Amenhotep III who was now deceased by a number of years so it is likely they were sent before the other nations learned of his death. But to get the complete picture, we need to keep a few things in mind.

To recap, during the reign of Amenhotep III, Egypt was no longer having to invade Palestine and Syria because these areas were conquered and subdued and set up as vassals states. Egyptian garrisons were stationed to maintain control. The mere threat of retaliation by the fierce Egyptian army was more than enough persuasion for them to cooperate.

The Hittites, Assyrians and Kassites (Babylonians) were at peace with Egypt because they were well acquainted with the powerful Egyptian army. While elsewhere the other nations continued to fight among themselves, they maintained a courteous and peaceful relationship with Egypt, paid tribute regularly and carried on correspondence with them.

These letters give detailed insight to the negotiations between rulers and the situation at the time. Sometimes, we have to read between the lines. Since some of the letters are addressed to Amenhotep III, I propose that they were received after his death and answered in his name by someone else because there are complaints about inferior gifts being sent to them compared to what had been sent in the past.

All of these things point to the time after the Exodus when Egypt was no longer full of her former wealth. The vast nation of the Israelites had taken a great deal of their gold and silver with them when they left.

The Hittites Begin to Make Their Move

Whereas earlier the foreign kings had all pledged their friendship with Egypt, after the Exodus revolt soon occurred. The Hittites began to invade Egyptian territories with the assistance of the Amurru (Amorites). The elders of Tunip wrote the pharaoh about the dangers of invasion and pleaded for assistance. In one letter, they state:

"For twenty years we have been sending to our lord, the king, the king of Egypt, but there has not come to us a word, no, not one."

This statement that they had been asking for help for 20 years but not receiving even a word is telling. This placed this letter, at the very least, 20 years after the Exodus.

The natural border between the Hittite land and Egypt was the small kingdom of the Amurru. In a treaty found in the Hittite capital, Suppululiumas recalls that he made a treaty with the Hurri king, Artatama, who was then threatened by the Mitanni king, Tushratta.

Going to the aid of the Hurri king, the Mitanni Tushratta flees and is then killed. The Hittite king then places one of Tushratta's sons as king of Mitanni and forms a treaty. With his power growing, the Hittite king then forms an alliance with the Amurru king, Aziru, who had been a faithful Egyptian vassal.

What all of this means is that because of the lack of Egyptian forces in her vassal states such as Syria and Palestine, the Hittites begin to make their move. After all, the Egyptian queen had written the Hittite king asking for a son of his to make him the pharaoh of Egypt. He had to know something was wrong in Egypt. This, plus the fact that his son was killed enroute to Egypt, must have fueled his anger against the Egyptians.

In the Amarna letters, this entire scenario is presented- the story is told of how alliances and treaties are gradually broken. Egyptian vassals in Canaan and Phoenicia wrote again and again for help.

Infighting among Egypt's Vassals

The Amurru prince, Abd-asrat, was accused by Rib-addi of Gebal of forming an alliance with the Babylonians and Mitanni. He requested troops from Egypt to help defend against them.

Later letters refer to his son, Aziru, as the leader of the Amurru who are also a great threat to the Egyptian vassals. Aziru wrote letters to the pharaoh protesting that he is faithful, but it is more than apparent that he is leading a great attack on the Phoenician cities, and even extending down into Canaan.

It became obvious to the writers of the frantic letters that no amount of pleading would result in the Egyptian pharaoh sending troops to help the vassals. It was a desperate situation for those in Phoenicia who were quickly losing ground to the Amurru, allies of the Hittites, as were the Mitanni (Hurrians/Horites). This presents a picture of exactly what would be expected of a superpower nation that had lost its king, wealth, and army.

In time, these leaders are told that the old king had died but the evidence shows that it was a period of time before this was done. It makes sense that they needed to stabilize the country and form an army before exposing their loss.

Letter from the Mitanni King to the dead Pharaoh

In EA 17, Tushratta writes to the pharoah Nimmuria, which has been transliterated to be "Neb-Maat-Re," one of Amernhotep III's names. He obviously did not know the king was now dead.

In this letter, he introduces himself and explains the circumstances of his rise to the throne. He then goes on to explain how, because the Pharoah had been friendly with his father, he was also extending his hand in friendship. This implies that those who were before him were hostile or at least a nuisance to Egypt. The following are excerpts from that letter:

"....When I ascended my father's throne, I was still young and Pihri did evil to my land and killed his lord. And therefore, he did not do me good nor him who was on friendly terms with me. I, however, especially because of those evils which were practiced in my land, made no delay(?), but the murderers of Artasumara, my brother, together with all that they had, I killed. Because you were friendly with my father, for this reason I sent and said to you:- "When my brother hears of it (these events) he will rejoice. My father was on friendly terms with you, and you were also on very friendly terms with my father. And my father, because you loved my sister, gave her to you,...

He goes on to explain that the Hittites have attacked and he won the battle. He listed the booty he was sending to pharaoh:

...,that my brother may know that [the army] of Hatti marched against my land, wholly as an enemy, and that Tishub, the lord, gave it into my hand, and that I have destroyed it. There was no one among them who returned to his own land.

Verily, a chariot and 2 horses, a boy and a girl, of the booty of the land of Hatti have I sent you.

As a present for my brother, 5 chariots, and a span of 5 horses, I have sent you.

And as a present for Giluhipa, my sister, a pair(?) of breast adornments of gold, a pair(?) of gold earrings, a mashu of gold, and a bottle full of good oil, I have sent her."

In another letter, EA 19, he seems to be responding to the first letter he has received from the pharoah since he wrote EA 17 and he refers to the pharaoh's request for his daughter to be his wife. Giluhipa (Gilukhepa) mentioned in the above letter, is his sister whom his father gave to Amenhotep III over 20 years earlier. In fact, she arrived the year of the Exodus and many details of the exchange were likely not finalized, such as gifts from the pharaoh.

This was a practice of Egypt as the reigning power- to ask for daughters of the foreign kings as a symbol of their friendship. But, as Egypt refused to reciprocate, it was likely also practiced as a means of leverage or insurance against insurrection.

Tushratta goes on to speak of all the gold which pharaoh had sent his father, and asks him to send even more which he can consider as the price for a wife. There is no doubt that at this time, this king is completely unaware that the pharaoh is deceased.

Tushratta is Angry at the Fake Gold He Received

In EA 20, it seems that more correspondence has taken place which we do not have access to. Tushratta complained about the gold which he had received from Egypt was not gold at all. Tushratta cannot understand this for he mentions that "in Egypt gold is more plentiful than dirt." He states that the pharaoh has imagined that he is angry at him but assures him that is not true.

Apparently, the pharaoh had complained that Tushratta's daughter has not been sent yet so Tushratta tries to placate him by saying he will send her in 6 months as he still has "work" to do for her, which implies preparing her for the event, or perhaps procrastinating and hoping for the gold he kept asking for.

It would only be a matter of time before Tushratta would learn that the emperor pharaoh, Amenhotep III, was dead. But it is obvious from these letters that the Egyptians tried to keep the secret as long as they could.

EA 26 was written by Tushratta to Tiye, the wife of Amenhotep III. Finally, it is apparent that he now knows Amenhotep III is no longer alive and Tiye's son is on the throne. He reiterates to Tiye his great love for her husband and that she knew how much he loved him.

Then he complains that her son has sent him statues of plated wood:

"Why have you [no]t exposed before Napb[urreya} the words that you yourself, and with your own mouth, said to [me]? If [you] do not expose them before him, and y[ou keep silent, can anyone [el]se know? Let [Nap]hurreya

*give me statues of sol[i]} gold! He must cause me no [dis]tress whatsoever, nor
[...]. Let him treat m[e] 10 times better [th]an his father did, [wi]th love and
evidence of esteem].*

In EA 29, Tushratta is now writing to Tiye's son, Akhenaton.
He seems to be trying to make the point that Akhenaton's father, Amenhotep
III, had made certain promises which this pharaoh isn't carrying out...

*"When [...], the father of Nimmureya, wrote to Artatama, my grandfather,
he asked for the daughter of [my grandfather, the sister] of my father. He
wrote 5, 6 times, but he did not give her. When he wrote my grandfather 7
times, then only under such pressure did he g[iv]e her. When Nimmureya, your
father, [wrote to Sutt[arna], m[y]father, and asked for my father's daughter, my
own sister, he wr[ote] 3, 4 times, but [he did not giv]e her. When he wrote 5, 6
times, only under such pressure did he g[iv]e [her]. W[hen] Nimmureya, [your
[fa]ther, wrote to me and asked for my daughter, I did [not] say n[o]. The [very]
first ti[me] I said [to] his messenger, "Of course I will give her."...*

*When [m]y [brother}, Nimmureya, went to his fate it was reported. [When
I heard} what was reported, [nothing] was allowed to be cooked in a pot. On
that day I myself wept,..."*

He further states in this letter how happy he was when he heard that the son
of Amenhotep III was now on the throne and how that was his only comfort.
He knew the pharaoh's mother, Tiye, was acquainted with how friendly their
relations had been.

But it seems that Amenhotep III had promised two gold statues at the time
Gilukhepa came to Egypt and the ones he received from the present pharaoh
were only wooden and Tushratta was not going to drop that subject.

The implication is that Amenhotep III was in the midst of arranging his
marriage with Tushratta's sister, Gilukhepa, when he was drowned in the Red
Sea. This is verified by a scarab he had issued, dated "year 10," the year of the
Exodus, about her coming to Egypt as his wife. Apparently she arrived with
her large entourage before all exchanges of payment were made.

The fact of the gold not being sent points to the situation Egypt found
herself in at that time. Gold, which was as "plentiful as dust" in Egypt,
suddenly became a much valued commodity since the children of Israel had
taken so much from them when they left.

When Tushratta received the plated wooden statues instead of the golden ones, he eventually sent his messengers who were instructed to seek an audience with the pharaoh. This posed a problem for Egypt and the messengers were detained for four years. This is indicative that a rather long time period was involved in stabilizing Egypt.

Biridiya of Megiddo

Megiddo had been the site of Thutmose III's first great victory and it had remained under Egyptian control since then. But now, letters arrived from the prince of Megiddo, Biridiya, that told how since the Egyptian archers had been recalled to Egypt, they were under attack:

*May the king, my lord, know that since the return (to Egypt) of the archers, Lab'ayu has waged war against me. We are thus unable to do the plucking: Ka-Zi-ra (harvesting),' and we are unable to go out of the city gate: fa-ag-ri because of Lab'ayu, When he learned that archers were not co[ming o]ut, he immediately [de]termined to take Magidda. May the king save his city lest Lab'ayu seize it. Look, the city is consumed by pestilence, by … So may the king give a garrison of 100 men to guard his city lest Lab'ayu seize it. Look, Lab'ayu has no other purpose. He seeks simply the seizure" of Magidda." (*EA 244)

Milkilu, Prince of Gezer

EA 271, was written by Milkilu, the prince of Gezer. The people of this town were obviously quite fearful of the situation. Also mentioned in this letter is Shuwardata, the prince of Hebron, located about 25 miles from Gibeon. Once again, the instability of the region is made clear. The Egyptian vassals were pleading for help:

"….Let the king know that powerful is the hostility against me and against Shuwardata. Let the king, my lord, protect his land from the hand of the `Apiru. If not, (then) let the king, my lord, send chariots to fetch us, lest our servants smite us."

Of interest is the request for chariots to rescue the prince and others(?) "lest our servants smite us." The people of the cities were greatly fearful. Again, this presents more evidence of the fact that Egypt's entire army had been lost except for those stationed in the vassal cities and they had been withdrawn back to Egypt. This left the cities which depended on Egypt to protect them from invaders now exposed and vulnerable.

Horemheb, General of the Army of Egypt

When Tutankhamun had been his father's appointed co-regent, a man by the name of Horemheb was chief administrator and commander-in-chief of the army. One of his first titles was "the royal spokesman for Egypt's foreign affairs."

He most certainly was overseeing vassal cities at the time of the death of the pharaoh, Amenhotep III in the Red Sea, because he survived when the entire army drowned. His titles were so elevated that it is believed that he was considered the heir-apparent to Tutankhamun if the young Tut failed to have a son before he died.

When the Egyptian disaster of the Exodus occurred, it was Horemheb who, already at the head of the military, reorganized and formed a new Egyptian army. He was most needed to head the army so there was no thought of him taking the post as pharaoh when Tutankhamun died.

There are many theories promoting a royal dispute between Ay and Horemheb as to who would take the throne when the young co-regent died and then the emperor Amenhotep III drowned. I believe the evidences show that Horemheb continued his role as general to save the country and there was no dispute. He was a faithful servant of Egypt and was compliant with Ay when he became the pharaoh for a few years.

When Akhenaton became the pharaoh, Horemheb continued as the commander of the army. Everyone in positions of power who remained alive after the Exodus had to cooperate if the country was going to survive. For this reason, I believe there was cooperation among those in control. This could have been a time of revolt but it wasn't. It was a time of survival and the evidence indicates a well planned organization of the government. But it likely would not have survived too long under the reign of Akhenaton.

Thankfully, it appears that Horemheb had a level head and was well versed in diplomacy. In his Memphite tomb, he included the claim that his name was "renown in the land of the Hittites."

But there were times when even Horemheb didn't know what to do. In the next Hittite text of Mursili son of Suppululiuma it speaks of "the man of Egypt, Arma'a" who I believe is Horemheb:

*"Then […] became hostile towards me, and Titti, [my servant] wrote [to] the ['ma]n' of Egypt (saying): '[Send] troops and chariots, and] … shall … me forth, and [I] will arise [and] come to the land of Egypt.' Then the troops and chariots of the land of Eg[ypt] came, and Titti arose and went to the land of [Eg]ypt. When, however, I wrote to <**Arma'a** (saying): '[Si]nce Tetti was m[y] servant, why then did you send your troops and chariots and [bring] him a[way]? Give my [serv] ant back to me!' [<**Arma'a**] did not give [him ba]ck [to me], nor did he [even wr]ite back to me. Then it came about that Zirtaya, [his] servant, wrote to me (saying): 'Sen[d] troops and chariots, and I will arise, and [come] to Hattusa.' So I sent troops and chariots, and they brought Zirt[aya, his servant], to Hattusa. Then <**Arma'a** w[rote] to me (saying): Since [Z]irtaya is my servant, [giv]e hi[m back to me]!' But I wrote back to him (saying): 'An[d you]? Wh[y] did you [not g] ive Tetti back to me?' Then <**Arma'a** remained totally quiet, [and] said [nothing] at all! [So] we were [not] on good terms with one another. We were [not] at all on [goo]d(?) terms."* ("Amarna Age Chronology and the Identity of Nibhururiya in the light of a Newly Reconstructed Hittite Text" by Jared L. Miller).

The explanation of why this name is believed to be Horemheb is given as:

"The plene writing of the name (Ar-ma-a, nom. Ar-ma-a-as), presumably an attempt to portray H/H /'armah/h /'a, or similar, recalls Haremhab's name as found in excerpts from Manetho, i.e. Armais, Harmais, Armesis and Armaios." (Miller)

The End of Amarna- "Evil Diseases of Egypt"

Although there are a lot of fragments of walls depicting the Amarna family, all we really know is that the last dated inscription of Akhenaton's reign is year 16. Scholars have settled on 17 years for his reign. This combined with the Amarna Letters comprises the bulk of what is known. Then everyone in Amarna seemed to disappear.

Evidence shows that the entire Amarna family suddenly disappeared at the same time. This mystery's answer can be found in the Bible.

*Deu. 7:15 And the LORD will take away from thee all sickness, and will put none of **the evil diseases of Egypt**, which thou knowest, upon thee; but will lay them upon all them that hate thee.*

*Deu. 28:27 The LORD will smite thee with **the botch of Egypt**, and with the emerods, and with the scab, and with the itch, whereof thou canst not be healed.*

Whatever these diseases were, we know for sure that they were fatal. Mursili, the son of Supiluliuma, in his "Plague Prayers", wrote a prayer to the Hittite storm god because of all the deaths in the Hatti land caused by a plague they got from the Egyptians prisoners:

"What is this that ye have done? A plague ye have let into the land. The Hatti land has been cruelly afflicted by the plague. For twenty years now men have been dying in my father's days, in my brother's days, and in mine own since I have become the priest of the gods....My father sent foot soldiers and charioteers who attacked the country of Amqa, Egyptian territory. Again he sent troops, and again they attacked it....The Hattian Storm-god, my lord, by his decision even then let my father prevail; he vanquished and smote the foot soldiers and charioteers of the country of Egypt. But when he brought back to the Hatti land the prisoners which they had taken, a plague broke out among the prisoners and they began to die.

When they moved the prisoners to the Hatti land, these prisoners carried the plague into the Hatti land. From that day on, people have been dying in the Hatti land." (Pritchard, pp. 394 and 395.)

The Hittites caught the plague from the Egyptian soldiers who were stationed in Amqa, Egyptian territory above Lebanon. And those who contracted the plague died including the great Suppiluliuma as well as his oldest son, Arnuwanda II who was being groomed to be the next king.

This plague was to have far-reaching consequences on many nations and kingdoms, preparing the region for the arrival of the children of Israel in Canaan, the promised land. The family of Akhenaton suddenly ceased to be in the ancient records and most certainly died of this terrible plague.

Egypt went from being the greatest world power to being almost completely destroyed. But it was not God's timing for it to come to end.

Chapter 16

END OF THE 18TH DYNASTY

With the Amarna family gone, a new pharaoh took the throne. The faithful servant of the empire, General Horemheb, arose to the position of emperor. There is no way to really know how many years it had been since the death of Amenhotep III and Tutankhamun, but a rough estimate can be made. According to the records available, Ay ruled for at least 4 or up to 10 years and Akhenaton's last known year was his regnal year 17. That is roughly 21 to 27 years since the Exodus. Horemheb would have been in his late 40's to mid 50's most likely.

The ancient records reveal that he most likely ruled for about 14 years and in that relatively short time, he spent his efforts attempting to restore Egypt. By the time Akhenaton's reign was over, Egypt was in a state of decay both physically and morally. State power had been centralized within the royal family and no provision made for the people of the land. The old gods of Egypt had been neglected and finally forgotten; there were no priests; the only officials over the common people were corrupt. The nation was dying out slowly. Horemheb began the process of restoring the grand Egypt he had known and fought for prior to the Exodus.

In his coronation inscription, obviously written after the fact, Horemheb had recorded for the ages all he had done for the nation:

"His majesty sailed down-stream as the image of Harakhte. Behold, he organized this land; he adjusted according to the time of Re. He restored the temples (from) the pools of the marshes to Nubia (T '-pdS t). He shaped all their images [in number] more than before, increasing the beauty in that which he made. Re rejoiced when he saw them, which had been found ruined aforetime. He raised up their temples. He fashioned 100 images with all (their) bodies correct, and with all splendid costly stones. He sought the precincts of the gods, which were in the districts in this land; he furnished them as they had been since the time of the first beginning. He established for them a daily

Wikimedia Commons- Captmondo/ CC BY-SA

Horemheb, the pharoah of restoration. He was the last pharaoh of the 18th Dynasty. He had been a general during the reign of Amenhotep III and vizier for his son Tutankhamun. He did not go with the pharaoh when he chased after the Israelites because he was in charge of the troops maintaining the vassals in Canaan, Syria and Lebanon and survived when the army was wiped out.

offering every day; all the vessels of their temples were wrought of silver and gold. He equipped them with priests, with ritual priests, and with the choicest of the army. He transferred to them lands and cattle, supplied with all equipment." (Ancient Records of Egypt Vol III The Nineteenth Dynasty, by James Henry Breasted, p. 18.)

On his stele at the foot of his Tenth Pylon at Karnak is recorded "The Great Edict of Horemheb." It is his decree to restore and re-establish order in Egypt. He issued judgements, laws and punishments. It presents a vivid picture of the degradation of Egypt in the years after the Exodus simply by the crimes listed. He covered crimes such as: robbing the poor of dues for the royal breweries and kitchens; robbing the poor of wood due the Pharaoh; unlawful appropriation of slave labor; dishonest inspectors conniving with tax collectors for a cut of the spoils; stealing of hides by soldiers and more.

The punishments are severe: for the stealing of hides, the penalty is a hundred blows, opening five wounds and taking from him by force the hides he stole. He was especially strict on deputies and officers and if any are accused of extortion, their nose shall be cut off and he will be sent to Tjaru (Tharu), the border fortress. These are just examples and give a clear picture of the corruption that was taking place.

He also searched for two honest men to act as judges, one in the north and one in the south. He was concerned about the poor, the common, and those who had nothing and did their best.

"…Then he seized palette and roll; he put it into writing according to all that his majesty, the king himself said. He spoke as follows: "[My majesty] commands … [concerning all] instances of oppression in the land.

If the poor man made for himself a craft with its sail, in order to be able to serve the Pharaoh, L.P.H., [loading it with the dues for the breweries and the kitchens of the Pharaoh, and he was robbed of the craft and] the dues, the poor man stood reft of his goods and stripped of his many labors. This is wrong, and the Pharaoh will suppress it by his excellent measures. If there be a [poor man] who pays the dues of the breweries and kitchens of the Pharaoh, L.P.H., to the two deputies, [and he be robbed of his goods and his craft, my majesty commands: that every officer who seizes the dues] and taketh the craft of any citizen of the army or of any person who is in the whole land, the law shall be executed against him, in that his nose shall be cut off, and he shall be sent to Tharu….

[Furthermore, my majesty commands that if any poor man be oppressed by] [robbe]ry, his cargo be emptied by theft of them, and the poor man stand reft of hi[s good]s, [no further exactions for dues shall be made from him] when he has nothing. For it is not good, this report of very great injustice. My majesty commands that restitution be made to him; behold .... .

I have improved this entire land ...... I have sailed it, as far as south of the wall, I have given ..., I have learned its whole interior, I have traveled it entirely in its midst, I have searched in .... [and I have sought two officials] perfect in speech, excellent in good qualities, knowing how to judge the innermost heart, hearing the words of the palace, the laws of the judgment-hall. I have appointed them to judge the Two Lands, to satisfy those who are in .... [I have given to each one] his seat; I have set them in the two great cities of the South and the North; every land among them cometh to him without exception; I have put before them regulations in the daily register [of the palace] .... I have directed [them] to the way of life; I led them to the truth, I teach them, saying: "Do not associate with others of the people; do not receive the reward of another, not hearing .... . How, then, shall those like you judge others, while there is one among you committing a crime against justice....

Hear ye these commands which my majesty has made for the first time governing the whole land, when my majesty remembered these cases of oppression which occur before this land." (Breasted Vol. III, pp. 25-33)

In his 7th regnal year, Horemheb reformed the Army and appointed priests of the various gods from upstanding men in the army to ensure they would be faithful to him and to Egypt. For the first time since the Exodus, the old gods of Egypt were brought back and their worship again instituted. He put the people to work through his many building projects including temples and other buildings. He built the 2nd, 9th and 10th Pylons of the Great Hypostyle Hall. It is because of Horemheb that we have more knowledge of the reign of Akhenaton because he reused blocks from Akhenaton's monuments in the building material for the 1st two pylons.

One of the most interesting inscriptions attributed to Horemheb tells how he instructed Maya, a highly favored official, to:

"...restore the burial of King Menkheprure (Thutmose IV), triumphant, in the august house on the west of Thebes." (Breasted, p. 19.)

This was written in ink in a lower chamber of Thutmose IV's tomb in Thebes. This was, in my opinion, the politically correct way to say "provide"

Inscription on the wall of Thutmose IV's tomb noting that Horemheb ordered Maya to "restore" the burial of Thutmose IV.

instead of "restore" a burial for the king since he had never been buried. He had drowned in the Red Sea and his body was never recovered. This is another circumstantial confirmation of the fact that the king who drowned did not have a funeral. Also of note, Horemheb chose to use his Thutmose IV name possibly because he was from Memphis where the king ruled by that name.

It can be observed in a study of the ancient mummies in the case where the actual body is not available, a substitute can be provided. The actual person was preferred but in cases where the original mummy is destroyed by bandits, substitutions were made. It was necessary to provide for those of the royal families, to make provisions for them in the afterlife. It is the same principle as the objects placed in young Tutankhamun's tomb by the Amarna family pertaining to their god, Aten.

Horemheb's Efforts to Restore Egypt

There is a stele that was found at Karnak that is termed "Tutankhamun's Restoration Stele." However, it cannot belong to him. It is dated to regnal year 1 in which Tutankhamun would have been about 9 to 10 years old. It can be seen that some names have been changed from Tutankhamun to Horemheb and for this cause it has been declared to have been originally

Tutankhamun's and thus usurped by Horemheb. I propose that it originally was a slab prepared in Tutankhamun's name in preparation for an inscription which never came to pass. I propose that Horemheb simply used this stele to place his own declaration on as it was already formed yet blank except for the top which featured the customary pictures of the pharaoh before the gods.

The language is similar to Horemheb's in his other stelae and inscriptions. On this stele it tells of some things the king has done and it presents a picture of Egypt recovering from the devastation after the Exodus. The description of the shrines being desolate, the gods having all turned their back on Egypt, and the army having had no success, all speak of chaos in the land. He also speaks of appointing priests which confirms that there were none:

"Now when his majesty appeared as king, the temples of the gods and goddesses from Elephantine [down] to the marshes of the Delta [had... and] gone to pieces. Their shrines had become desolate, had become mounds overgrown with [weeds]. Their sanctuaries were as if they had never been. Their halls were a footpath. The land was topsy-turvy, and the gods t¬¬urned their backs upon this land. If [the army was] sent to Djahi to extend the frontiers of Egypt, no success of theirs came at all. If one prayed to a god to seek counsel from him, he would never come [at all]. If one made supplication to a goddess similarly, she would never come at all….

Then his majesty made monuments for the gods, [fashioning] their cult-stat-ues of genuine fine gold from the highlands, building their sanctuaries anew as monuments for the ages of eternity, established with possessions forever, setting for them divine offerings as a regular daily observance, and provisioning their food offerings upon earth. He surpassed what had been previously, [he] went beyond what had [been done] since the time of the ancestors. He has inducted priests and prophets from the children of the nobles of their towns, (each) the son of a known man, whose (own) name is known. He has increased their [property] in gold, silver, bronze, and copper, without limit in [any respect]. He has filled their workhouses with male and female slaves, the product of his majesty's capturing [in every foreign country]. All the [property] of the temples has been doubled, tripled, and quadrupled in silver, [gold], lapis lazuli, turquoise, every (kind of) august costly stone, royal linen, white linen, fine linen, olive oil, gum, fat, … incense, benzoin, and myrrh, without limit to any good thing…" Ancient Near Eastern Texts Relating to the Old Testament, by Pritchard, p.251-2.)

A most fascinating inscription comes from the "Vienna Fragment." It depicts a group of Egyptian officials bowing to the superior, Horemheb, although his figure is lost. He is giving them instructions concerning a group of Asiatics whose town has been plundered and destroyed. They are making a request to settle in the land and pasture their herd "after the manner of your father's fathers since the beginning...", a very interesting parallel to the story of Joseph:

"--------Asiatics; others have been placed in their abodes --------- they have been destroyed, and their town laid waste, and fire has been thrown ---------- ---- they have come to entreat the Great in Strength to send his mighty sword before ----------Their countries are starving, they live like goats of the mountain, [their] children ---------- saying: "A few of the Asiatics, who knew not how they should live, have come [begg]ing [a home in the domain] of Pharaoh, L. P. H., after the manner of your fathers' fathers since the beginning, under ------------. Now, the Pharaoh, L. P. H., gives them into your hand, to protect their borders." (Breasted, p. 7)

This is another absolute confirmation of the policy of Joseph's pharaoh being called upon to allow them to relocate in Egypt. Once a king, or pharaoh, had issued a decree, it was upheld by later kings. This is why the Israelites were not expelled from Egypt when the Hyksos were expelled. But Ahmose got around this command by having them enslaved.

Horemheb apparently dedicated his entire life to the welfare of Egypt, serving under pharaohs Tutankhamen, Ay and Akhenaton and finally becoming the pharaoh himself. But, like several earlier kings, he did not have a son to succeed him as Pharaoh. He appointed his vizier, Paramesse, to succeed him to the throne upon his death. This man was of non-royal birth, from the Nile Delta region and was obviously extremely capable and faithful. When Horemheb died, this man became Rameses I, the founder of the 19th Dynasty.

Horemheb was a very great pharaoh. He cared for his country and he cared for the people. He restored justice mixed with mercy as is seen in his Great Edict. He was respected by the foreign nations. Because of him, Egypt survived and began to thrive again. The God of Abraham had allowed Egypt to survive, at least for awhile, as a still great power.

Chapter 17

THE ROYAL MUMMIES

A discussion of the ancient mummies is necessary at this point, not only considering Horemheb's order to "renew" the burial of Thutmose IV, but also considering my contention that some of the pharaohs listed as separate people are actually the same person in two different positions as pharaoh. This is a central feature of Ron's belief concerning the 18th Dynasty and a hallmark of this reconstruction.

At death, the Egyptians believed that a body was necessary for the ba, the ka and the akh to survive. These were, loosely translated, the various "spirit forms" which made up the psychic person and survived after death. However, in cases where the person was unavailable for burial, etc., any available body would suffice as long as it was labeled with the name of the deceased. They believed that as long as a person's name was being spoken or was on the walls of his tomb, his immortality was assured. The name was the most important factor.

"The tomb, the mummy, the equipment, the paintings and reliefs were all designed to help preserve the name of the individual. The greatest horror was to have your name destroyed, cut out from a wall." ("Mummies, Myth and Magic in Ancient Egypt" by Christine El Mahdy, p. 13.)

If the mummy of the actual individual was so vital, why would they fear the desecration of their name? Because it was the key, according to their belief in their immortality. The mummy was important, as were the statues of the deceased. But the mummy could be supplied in a situation where one was not available at their death.

Since it was considered a sacred duty of each king to protect the burials of his ancestor-kings, if a king couldn't find a mummy for a particular king, he would provide one.

However, the mummy remaining in the tomb must not have been all that important due to a discovery made in 1881. Tomb 320 (TT320) was discovered near Deir el Bahri. It contained mummified remains and funerary equipment of over 50 kings, queens, and other high officials of Egypt.

The mummies were brought to this tomb during the 21st Dynasty to perhaps protect them from tomb robbers, but they didn't succeed. The two Abd er Rassul brothers had originally discovered the tomb and had been selling objects from the tomb for a number of years. When authorities finally discovered the tomb after objects began to appear on the market, they discovered it was full of torn mummy cloth and mummies in the wrong coffins. Some of the limbs and even heads of some mummies were separated from the bodies.

Although Thutmose III and Amenhotep II are the same man, there have been found mummies for each name. This does not make void Ron's assertion that the Amenhoteps and Thutmoses were the same people in different positions. I propose that the later kings and even later dynasties did their best to supply a mummy for each name if they were unable to find one.

Amenhotep I's Mummy- Authentic

G. Elliot Smith- Public Domain

The sarcophagus and mummy of Amenhotep I.

Amenhotep I's mummy was never unwrapped because it was in such good condition. It was instead x-rayed and it revealed several genetic peculiarities which were shared by the mummies of several of his ancestors.

The most obvious of these peculiarities was the fact that he had a type of malocclusion - a prominent protrusion of the top front teeth like an overbite. This genetic feature was seen in all his female relatives- sister, mother, grandmother and daughter. It is likely that his mummy is accurately identified.

Thutmose I's Mummy- Fraud

But many of the others found in the cache were of doubtful identification. The evidence shows the mummy of Thutmose I to be extremely doubtful and of course, I believe it to be impossible. It is known that he ruled at least 21 years under that name:

G. Elliot Smith- Public Domain

The mummy identified as Thutmose I. It is an obvious fraud, supplied perhaps by well-meaning people of the 21st Dynasty.

"However, several eminent physical anthropologists who have seen these x-rays have been absolutely convinced that this mummy is that of a young man, perhaps 18 years of age, certainly not over twenty." "X-Raying the Pharaohs" by James E. Harris and Kent R. Weeks, (1973) p.131-2.

The fact that this mummy is far too young to be this king is evidence enough. When x-rayed, they discovered this mummy's arms were at his side, not crossed on his chest as pharaohs' normally were. His identification was originally based on the fact that he resembled other mummies:

"Among the mummies discovered at Deir-el-Bahari was one, which on account of its having been found in a coffin bearing the name of Pinozen I of the XXIst Dynasty, was formerly supposed to be the mummy of that king. Maspero, however, formed the opinion that it was the mummy of Thutmoses I on account of the facial resemblance which it bore to the Pharaohs Thutmoses II and III" "Egyptian Mummies" by G. Elliot Smith and Warren R. Dawson (1924) p. 91.

Thutmose II's Mummy- Fraud

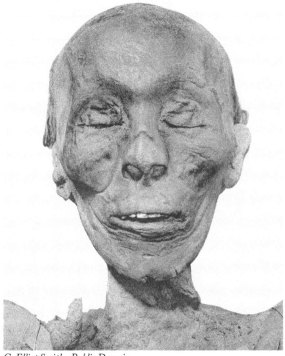

G. Elliot Smith- Public Domain

The mummy said to be Thutmose II contained a label with his name misspelled and the dating of its "rewrapping" in the 21st Dynasty. The age of the man was said to be about 30 years old by Elliot Smith and 25-30 by others. This mummy was substituted by the 21st dynasty when they couldn't find a mummy for Thutmose II.

They obviously believed he had once reigned which coincides with my belief that, as Moses, the royal family simply portrayed him as having died rather than letting the true story be known. When they could find no tomb, much less a mummy, they felt it was their duty to supply one.

Thutmose III's Mummy- Fraud

The mummy said to be Thutmose III was also determined to be too young to be the long reigning monarch. In addition, he was just barely five feet 3 inches tall (a little taller since his feet were broken off). This is certainly not the picture of the Napoleon of Egypt, as he was later referred to be.

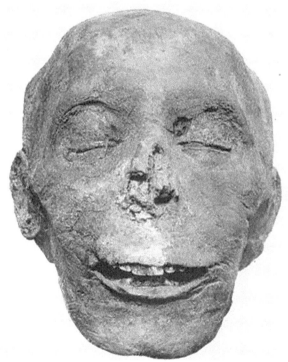

G. Elliot Smith- Public Domain

The mummy said to be Thutmose III.

This issue has caused nothing but confusion. When a cache of over 50 kings and queens was found in 1881, this should have sent up many red flags. In addition, the methods of mummification differed significantly from the method used in the 18th Dynasty.

The resemblance of the three Thutmoses causes me to wonder how they obtained so many people who resembled each other to provide mummies.

However, I believe there are a few mummies that are authentic.

Amenhotep II's Mummy- Authentic

The mummy of Amenhotep II, the same pharaoh as Thutmose III, was discovered in his own tomb in 1898 by Victor Loret. Unfortunately, men hired to guard the tomb later plundered his tomb and his body was badly damaged.

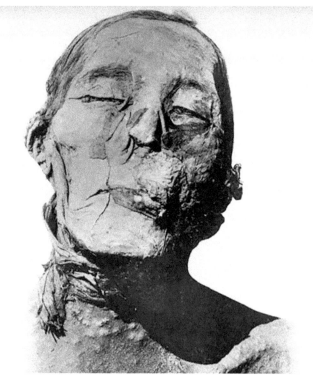

Public Domain

The mummy of Amenhotep II. He was found in his own tomb in 1898. His body was damaged by looters but it still revealed a great deal of evidence that supports this being the authentic mummy of this king.

Public Domain

Estimates placed his age at between 40 and 50 years. However, his hair was gray, he had a bald spot on the back of his head and he had degenerative arthritis, usually seen in people aged 60 and over. This is feasible as he ruled 30 years as Amenhotep II plus three years as Thutmose III when he assumed his reign in year 23 of Hatshepsut. Since he was 18 years old when he came to the throne, this would make him approximately 51 years old.

Thutmose IV's Mummy- Obvious Fraud

The one to take a special look at is the one for whom Horemheb told his official to "renew his burial"- Thutmose IV. His mummy was not found in his own tomb but was found in a cache of mummies in the tomb of Amenhotep II.

When examined, he was discovered to be a very emaciated man, perhaps 25-28 years old. His height was 5 feet 4.8 inches with his feet broken off. His arms were crossed over his chest like other pharaohs which points to the possibility that Horemheb had another man mummified to fill in for Thutmose IV, if this is the mummy he supplied, because this was clearly not him.

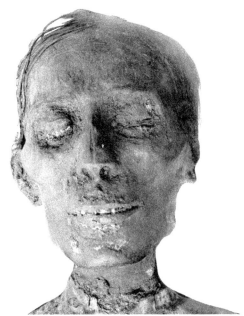

G. Elliot Smith- Public Domain
The mummy said to be Thutmose IV.

Amenhotep III's Mummy- Fraud

A mummy for Amenhotep III was also found and it was badly damaged and the head had been broken off. The lid of the coffin containing this mummy bore the name of Sety II while the coffin box belonged to Ramesses III. These facts alone are suspect and indicate a mummy was supplied after the fact.

Examination showed this man to be obese with serious dental problems and almost completely bald. He displayed abscessed teeth with heavy tartar.

In addition to this, the researchers discovered that the process used during the mummification employed a resinous material that turned out to be radiopaque, which meant clear x-rays could not be obtained.

It was not possible to determine his age. This mummy, obviously a fraud, was the origin of the belief that Amenhotep III became obese and in ill health in his later years.

Public Domain   *Public Domain*

The mummy labeled Amenhotep III.

But the most important fact to take note of about the mummy said to be Amenhotep III is that the mummification process used on this mummy was not used until the 21st and 22nd Dynasties. This is an obvious case of a mummy being supplied when one did not exist.

Hatshepsut's Family's Mummies- Authenic

A project began in 1966 at the University of Michigan's School of Dentistry sponsoring the x-raying of a number of Egyptian mummies in hopes of ascertaining biologic relationships between members of the royal families of ancient Egypt, among other things.

Fortunately, a number of mummies of Hatshepsut's family were found in a state that allowed positive identification. The ones not in question of being supplied or erroneous are those of females as there would be no reason to supply a mummy for a non-pharaoh. In marriages among siblings which produce offspring, genetic traits will be passed through many generations. Some of those include the following with their relationship to Hatshepsut:

- Ahmose-Meryet-Amon, wife of Amenhotep I (Hatshepsut's mother)
- Ahmose-Nefertiry, the wife of Ahmose (Hatshepsut's grandmother)
- Ahhotep, the wife of Seqenenre-Tao II (her great-grandmother)
- Tetisheri, the wife of Senakhtenre-Tao (her great-great-grandmother)

All of the females were x-rayed except Ahhotep, Hatshepsut's great-grand-mother. They discovered a remarkable trait among these related women. The following quotes are from "X-Raying the Pharaohs" by James E. Harris and Kent R. Weeks, copyright 1973, which gives an account of the results of that project:

"The lateral x-ray of Ahmose I's queen, Ahmose-Nefertiry, reveals the prominent protrusion already observed in Tetisheri and other early New Kingdom rulers and their families. The facial skeleton and the teeth provide a method by which family relationships can be evaluated." (P.31)

Like her grandmother, Tetisheri, she [Ahmose-Nefertiry] was noticeably bald and wore strands of hair twisted with her own to hide that fact.... The marked maxillary protrusion (buck teeth) noted in the mummy of Tetisheri was even more pronounced in her granddaughter, suggesting a rather close relationship, since the tendency toward malocclusion has been considered a genetic characteristic." (P. 128).

"Buck teeth, called Class II malocclusions by orthodontists, are common in the United States but rare in Egypt,..." (P. 65)

"One of the wives-sisters of Amenhotep I, Ahmose-Meryet-Amon, was also x-rayed. She showed a pattern of dentition similar to that of her husband-brother and to that of the women of her family, Tetisheri and Nefertiry, who preceded her." (P. 130.)

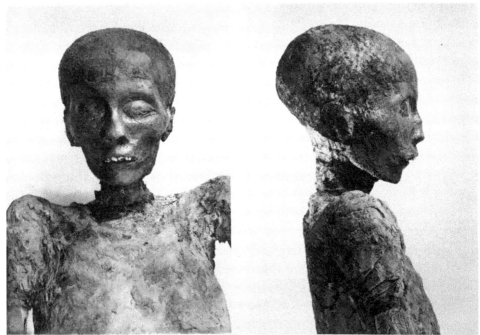

G. Elliot Smith– Public Domain
Ahmose-Meryet-Amon, the mother of Hatshepsut.

Another trait was also noted in Amenhotep I, whom I believe to be Hatshepsut's father (also, the same person as Thutmoses I whom scholars believe to be a separate individual)

"Like his predecessors, he [Amenhotep I] had a pronounced chin". (P. 130)

In 1988, I had been studying the data on a particular mummy found in 1898 by Victor Loret in a side chamber of the tomb of Amenhotep II along with two other mummies, all three lying side by side with no coffins. They had obviously been brought here from their own tombs in antiquity and plundered of all funerary items. I believed there was a possibility it was Hatshepsut, herself.

G. Elliot Smith- Public Domain
Ahmose-Nefertiry, the grandmother of Hatshepsut.

Public Domain
The three mummies found in Amenhotep II's tomb. The Elder Lady is on the left.

These mummies were not in coffins. There was no precedent for providing mummies of family members. These were simply moved from most likely their own tombs to this tomb to protect the mummies from tomb robbers who had no problem with destroying mummies.

The mummy I was interested in was that of a woman dubbed the Elder Lady. One feature particularly attracted my interest- her left arm was frozen in position across her chest, her left hand still in a clench as if she had been holding a scepter. Only the physical daughter of the pharaoh was technically entitled to such a royal burial. In addition, her case was special in the sense that she had been elevated to the position of royal heir for the purpose of allowing for the pharaonic line to continue.

Therefore, I believed it is more than likely that this was Hatshepsut. Although her two tombs were known, no mummy had ever been found. In addition, this mummy was found in the tomb of Amenhotep II, the last pharaoh of her lifetime.

I was not the only person to notice that this elder lady bore a resemblance to the early relatives of Hatshepesut:

"The face of the elder woman (n61070) presents an undoubted likeness to Nofritari;…" (The Royal Mummies, by G. Elliot Smith, p. 41)

Nofritari was the wife of Ahmose, the father of Hathsepsut's father. This meant she was Hatshepsut's grandmother.

It is my belief that the early mummies of the 18th Dynasty were preserved and accurate, including the mummy of Hatshepsut, even though her name is not on the mummy. Her father's mummy was buried as Amenhotep I. Mummies for Thutmose I, Thutmose II and Thutmose III were supplied at a later date. Their resemblance to each other indicates they were obviously members of the same family.

Unfortunately, there have been recent DNA testing of some mummies even though it is still debated among scientists how accurate they can be. I have read so many claims that the DNA tests on ancient mummies are reliable and equally as many articles arguing against it. It is known that testing on ancient mummies results in only part of the entire DNA.

One of those tested was the Elder Lady whom I am convinced is the mummy of Hatshepsut. Their conclusion was that this mummy is the mother of Tutankhamun, Queen Tiye.

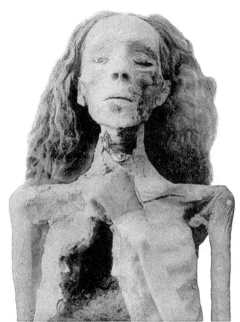

G. Elliot Smith- Public Domain
The "Elder Lady" that I believe is Hatshepsut.

The familial resemblances with her known family members is so pronounced, that I am of the opinion they have made a mistake in their identification. The two genetic features the Elder Lady shares with the other members of Hatshepsut's family cannot be discounted.

In conclusion, the study of the ancient mummies cannot be relied upon. Very few were found in their own tombs. Many, many had been unwrapped and damaged with body parts broken off, etc. They were found in caches with large numbers of other mummies in coffins and sarcophagi with the names of other people.

The one mummy we can have confidence in is the mummy of Tutankhamun and it was damaged profoundly during the hurried mummification process which caused his body to literally combust.

Chapter 18

THE BATTLE FOR MOUNT SINAI

While Egypt struggled during the year after the Exodus, the children of Israel journeyed to Mount Sinai in present day Saudi Arabia. It was at this holy mountain that God organized His people for the great task that laid ahead for them.

After the dispersion from the tower of Babel, the people had spread out in the world according to their language groups. Paganism was the norm and knowledge of the True Creator was dying out in most areas. Truth was corrupted and had God not intervened, all knowledge of Him could have easily been lost. A safe haven had been provided to the children of Israel in Egypt where they would grow and prosper.

As time neared for their further organization into the nation that would take the knowledge of the God of Abraham to the world, God allowed them to be enslaved. He then led them out of slavery through His servant Moses, but there was still a fiery furnace they had to pass through. From that point forward, their lives would not be easy. But they had miracle after miracle worked on their behalf to refine and teach them.

The journey across what is now known as the Sinai Peninsula was long, hot and difficult. But God sent a cloud to protect them from the sun and he provided Divine assistance as He said "I bare you on eagles' wings" in Exodus 19:4:

Exo. 13:17 And it came to pass, when Pharaoh had let the people go, that God led them not through the way of the land of the Philistines, although that was near; for God said, Lest peradventure the people repent when they see war, and they return to Egypt: 18 But God led the people about, through the way of the wilderness of the Red sea: and the children of Israel went up harnessed out of the land of Egypt. 19 And Moses took the bones of Joseph with him: for he had straitly sworn the children of Israel, saying, God will surely

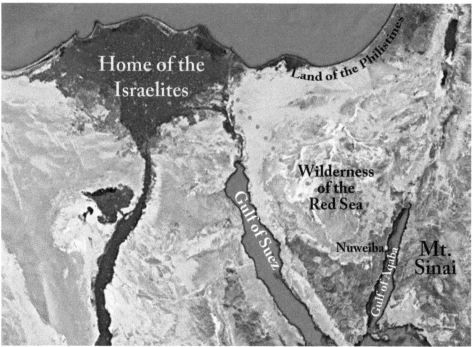

Google Earth

visit you; and ye shall carry up my bones away hence with you. 20 And they took their journey from Succoth, and encamped in Etham, in the edge of the wilderness. 21 And the LORD went before them by day in a pillar of a cloud, to lead them the way; and by night in a pillar of fire, to give them light; to go by day and night: 22 He took not away the pillar of the cloud by day, nor the pillar of fire by night, from before the people.

The Biblical story of the Exodus is full of miracles which cannot be explained in natural terms. As seen in the evidences presented thus far of the events in Egypt up to the Exodus and its aftermath in Egypt, the miracles are not presented as such in the historical records. The miraculous nature of the events have to be seen in the resulting ancient records. For many people, they cannot accept these miracles without another witness to the events which spell out the same events in the same context. But it doesn't happen like that most of the time.

Just as in Biblical times, there were true miracles involved in Ron's discovery of the holy mountain as well as tragedies. Fortunately, these events were well documented and the miraculous nature is evident. It is by an examination of the events associated with the revelation of the real Mount

Sinai that it becomes obvious that God revealed it, not any man.

At this time, I will present the events leading to Ron's determination of the real Mount Sinai as well as the difficulties encountered. The story must be told to reveal the Divine origin of the discovery. Just as Moses had to write about himself in the Scriptures he authored, Ron's story reveals human effort guided by Divinity. His human errors, like Moses', sometimes brought suffering. But eventually, when it was God's time, Ron's persistence paid off.

The Discovery of the Real Mount Sinai

Ron believed the commonly accepted location for Mount Sinai in the Sinai Peninsula was incorrect. In 1978, he believed Mount Sinai was across the Gulf of Aqaba in Saudi Arabia because of seeing the chariot remains. All he had were flight maps and even they were difficult to get of that region.

He determined the mountain he believed to be the correct one based on one major factor- in front of this mountain was an ancient volcanic rim which enclosed an area he estimated to be approximately 5,000 acres, enough room for the entire camp of Israel to live safe from outside interference. It also was within the area of Midian.

He knew he had to go there and see for himself. But after almost five years of applying to the Saudi Embassy for a visa, he was met with stony silence. In December of 1983, he made a fateful decision- he would enter illegally from the Jordanian border.

Ron had taken his two sons to Israel and slowly made his way to Jordan, stopping at Petra and various interesting locations before arriving at the border.

Satellite image of the area in front of a mountain that is compassed by a volcanic rim of black mountains. It is roughly 6 miles by 10 miles. Although there are some hills within this area, there still is a vast area. This would have been more than enough for the great multitude.

NASA

Google Earth
Nuweiba beach seen at near top left red dot. Right bottom is the large whitish bean-shaped area Ron believed could have been the camp of the Israelites. The smaller area to the right of that is the area he believed might have been the camp for those who were not members of the children of Israel called the mixed multitude who couldn't live in the main camp.

He had told only two people of his plan, not even his two sons. One was Jim Irwin, Apollo 15 astronaut and the eighth person to walk on the moon. Ron met Col. Irwin in Turkey when he was searching for Noah's Ark on Mt. Ararat while Ron was working on another mountain. The other person Ron told was a friend who had worked with him who will remain unnamed. No one within his family knew of his plan. He had learned it was best to keep his plans private until he returned. He would soon learn how true that was.

After over four years of trying to get a visa, Ron believed this was all he could do. It never crossed his mind that it could get him in so much trouble.

Nathan Bange
Viewing the mountain, Jebel Maqla, in the Jebel el Lawz range.

Illegal Entry

Arriving at the Jordanian border, Ron told his sons to wait for him while he crossed the border in the middle of the night. But the boys would not hear of it. They insisted on coming and he felt he had no choice but to allow Danny and Ronnie to come. He had inquired as to what would happen to someone who was caught in Saudi illegally. He was told that the person would be immediately escorted to the border and kicked out.

The crossing was relatively simple and without complication. They parked their rental car in a lot close to the official border crossing. They waited until the early hours of pre-dawn and strolled across after walking down from the border crossing near Haql.

They first tried to make their way to the Gulf of Aqaba and hoped to snorkel and see if there were any visible artifacts in the water. But that was taking too much time and Ron decided it was more important to go to the mountain.

Hailing a taxi on the main road from Haql, they had the driver take them where Ron showed him on the map. Ron had him drive east to enter into the mountain range from the north. In time, the driver said he could go no further.

The road had ended and they had entered into the unpaved rocky and bumpy area within the mountains. The driver then found them a small truck and driver who drove them the rest of the way while the taxi was to wait for them on the main road.

The language barrier presented issues and thankfully, Ron had the map. When he recognized they should be at or near the location, he had the driver slow down. As he surveyed the mountain in front of him, he saw that the top of the mountain was black. He thought of the Scripture that talked about the mountain being on fire from the presence of God. It certainly looked to him as if it were burnt.

He motioned to the driver and had him turn into the area at the foot of the mountain. There he saw a number of round, white marble pieces lying around what Ron believed was a very large altar with what looked like a corral.

Randall Lee
The first view of Jebal Maqla in the Jebel el Lawz range that Ron believed was Mount Sinai. The blackened mountain top was one feature which Ron noticed. The area Ron was looking for was just beyond the ridge to the left.

Viveka Pontén
White marble pieces scattered in front of the long, chevron-shaped altar structure.

Randall Lee
Standing in the large area Ron believed was a man-made dried up lake bed.

There was a large depression in front of this area that clearly looked like a dried up, man-made lake. Because of this depression, there was only one way into the large area at the foot of the mountain where these objects were located.

Then, out of seemingly nowhere, a Datsun 4-wheel drive truck pulled up and a lot of angry exchanges were made between their driver and the man in the Datsun. The local police had been called by someone and they were told to leave immediately. Ron photographed all he could as quickly as he could before this exchange and he was disappointed but thankful that he had gotten to see all that he had seen.

Speeding back the way they came, the truck met back up with the waiting taxi and they went back to the border. Everything seemed to be going well until they were in line to go through the border check point. They couldn't sneak out as they had entered because they were told to leave immediately and it was still daylight. They simply lined up with everyone else.

Charged with Espionage

When Ron presented his passport expecting a tough chewing out, they were instead brusquely arrested and quickly taken to Haql where they were placed in jail. There they were told they were being charged with espionage for the State of Israel. They were not allowed to make any telephone calls.

When first questioned, they asked Ron what he did for a living and he told them he was an anesthetist. They did not know what that meant even though they had English-speaking interrogators. So Ron tried to explain it simply and said he was a sleep doctor, that he put people to sleep for surgery. At that point, the interrogator stopped the questioning and told him they were experiencing a plague in the jail and surrounding compound and asked him if he could help.

They explained that the men would get high fevers, severe abdominal distress, body aches and some developed delirium and finally died. The first thing Ron did was write a prescription for antibiotics which was honored at the pharmacy. Ron was acutely aware that the whole area was infested with mosquitoes which he hated until his last breath. He figured the plague was something mosquito-born, most likely yellow fever.

He next asked for as many liters of olive oil they could get. They couldn't figure out what he needed that for but they provided all he needed. He poured it into all the primitive hole-in-the-ground latrines. Next he had them find all standing water in the area and pour enough oil in the water to completely cover the water with a film.

This immediately killed all the mosquito larvae in the water. He told the men to kill all the mosquitoes they could and try to avoid any bites. From that point, with everyone on antibiotics, there were no new cases of the mysterious sickness and all those who were sick recovered.

This bought some good will for the prisoners but not enough to get them released. Day after day, they were brought in one at a time and interrogated. Ron told them the details of what he saw at the mountain in the Jebel el Lawz range and explained how it confirmed the details in both the Bible and the Koran.

Chief interrogator, Abukahlet, then sent a team to the mountain to investigate. When they returned, they told him they found nothing. This was sent in a report directly to the king. The Saudis were obviously concerned about having Americans imprisoned, especially when they were charged with being Israeli spies. They were checking out their story as best they could.

At times, Ron said it looked so bleak he never imagined they would ever be released. He was desperately worried about his boys who were in their early 20's. Daily they kept telling the authorities they were simply explorers looking for Mount Sinai and their belief that Moses had led the people across the Gulf of Aqaba. Day after day, this continued to their chagrin. There was a radar station nearby in the mountain range which most likely added credibility to the charge but he didn't know about the radar station until much later.

There were some among their jailers who believed they were telling the truth. Unfortunately, the ones who didn't believe him wielded more power.

But something happened that seemed to change everything. The interrogators came to Ron one day and said for him to come with them. Ron was taken to a

Saudis are holding son, grandsons of Kentuckian

By Jack Brammer
Herald-Leader Frankfort bureau

LIVINGSTON — Ronald Eldon Wyatt displayed an adventurous spirit at an early age, his father, Hobert William Wyatt, recalled yesterday.

Today, his 52-year-old son and two grandsons are being held prisoners in Saudi Arabia while Wyatt, 73, and his wife, Lottie, 71, anxiously await their return.

The three were captured earlier this year, apparently after straying from an archaeological search in Jordan, Wyatt said.

"They had visas for Jordan but not for Saudi Arabia," he said. "They left the United States on Jan. 20 to search and deep-sea dive in Jordan for religious artifacts. They told us they would be back on Feb. 6. A week after they they didn't show up, we called the State Department and they told us they were in prison in Saudi Arabia."

Ronald Eldon Wyatt and his two sons, Danny, 24, and Ronnie, 22, are three of about 2,-000 Americans now in custody overseas, said Richard Weeks, a spokesman for the State De-partment in Washington.

"We are aware of the Wyatt case and can confirm that we are working for their release from prison in Saudi Arabia," Weeks said yesterday. "But we cannot release any more information because no waiver of the privacy act has been signed by the prisoners or family members."

Last month, the Kentucky General Assembly passed a resolution sponsored by Rep. Danny Ford, R-Mount Vernon, requesting that the State Deparment and Kentucky's congressional delegation assist in securing the release of Ronald Wyatt and his sons from the Saudi Arabian prison.

U.S. Sen. Wendell Ford and U.S. Rep. Hal Rogers have informed the Wyatts that they are working on their son's behalf.

Wyatt's 10 other children are participating in efforts to release Ronald and his sons.

"One of my other boys and two daughters are at his place near Nashville, calling up Washington and whoever else we can to get them back home," he said yesterday from his home in southern Rockcastle County.

(Turn to SAUDIS, back page)

April 10, 1984 from the Lexington Herald-Leader, Lexington, Kentucky. Ron's family knew nothing about where they were until his father, Hobart, contacted his congressmen.

helicopter and told to get in. Three of the men climbed into the helicopter and told Ron to show them where Moses and the great multitude crossed the sea. They obviously thought this would trip Ron up and further show his story to be fictitious.

Ron directed the pilot south down the beach. As the helicopter headed south, it made a short detour into the rugged mountains just east of the beach. Ron said the helicopter began to descend and then hovered over an open area where it paused close enough to see the ground clearly. One of the men told Ron to look closely and there below them was a mass of bleached bones. The warning was given that this could be him and his sons if he didn't tell them the truth. Needless to say, Ron assured him he was telling them the truth.

The helicopter again ascended and followed the beach until Ron told them to land opposite Nuweiba which was easily visible. *"Why would Musa bring the people here?"*- they kept asking. As Muslims, they believed in Moses but were adamant that he didn't bring the people there. They refused to even listen to the idea that Mount Sinai could be in their country. They clearly wanted it to remain in the Sinai Peninsula. Ron said his interrogators were frightening, especially to his sons.

The Column

When they landed, there on the beach was a large column. It contained writing which Ron recognized as Archaic Hebrew. The interrogators also recognized this as Jewish writing. In this barren and uninhabited region, the column still stood tall after thousands of years. No one knew of its existence until that helicopter landed where Ron had pointed, opposite Nuweiba.

Ron then told them he had found a matching column on the Nuweiba beach whose inscriptions had been eroded away as it laid on its side in the surf. The men took numerous photos of the column and talked excitedly among themselves in Arabic. Things changed from that point on. He believed without a doubt that column had saved his life.

Randall Lee

Today a marker is set in concrete on the shore in Saudi Arabia where the column the men saw when they landed the helicopter where Ron told them to set down.

The column Ron found lying in the surf on the south part of the beach at Nuweiba. The part lying in the water had eroded and if any inscriptions were there, they were now gone. He told the local authorities about the column and they had the column moved to the side of the main road opposite where it was found and set in concrete.

Mary Nell Lee

But this wasn't enough to calm his youngest son, Ronnie, who wasn't handling the situation very well. He told his father he was going to make a break for it, that he couldn't handle being there any longer. Ron tried to reason with him but to no avail. He was mentally unable to continue any longer.

When Ron realized how serious Ronnie was, the three of them agreed to make a break. Ron couldn't let him go alone even though he knew it would mean they would all be shot if they were caught. A plan had to made. Ron reasoned that the best time to make their attempted escape would be on a Thursday night when the Moslems were preparing for their holy day to began. It was agreed that the next Thursday night would be the time.

As Thursday neared, they learned a very troubling bit of news. There was a guard named Ali who had been particularly kind to them all. They were very fond of him and it was Ali who had been assigned to guard them Thursday night. Ron told the boys they couldn't do it while Ali was on duty. Ali would be severely punished and most likely shot if they escaped. The Saudis were not very forgiving of dereliction of duty. Fortunately, Ronnie agreed to wait until the next Thursday.

The next Wednesday, all thoughts were on the next day and their planned escape. Then the most unexpected thing happened. The head of the prison compound came to their barren room and told them it was over- they were going home. No explanations were given. They had been imprisoned for 75 days with no contact with the outside world. The worst part was that all Ron's film was confiscated.

They needed no preparations to get ready. All they had were their clothes and a tattered old deck of cards the guards had pulled together from odd pieces and gave them which Ron brought home with him.

It was finally over! He breathed a prayer of supreme gratitude. He admitted he was not comfortable at the thought of an escape attempt.

Supreme Betrayal

When they were finally released and debriefed before being allowed to fly home, they spent three days in Jordanian custody while arrangements were made. It was at this time they were told that Ron's friend whom he had confided in of his plan to sneak into Saudi had made a call to the Saudi Embassy in Washington D.C. and accused the Wyatts of being Israeli spies. The Saudis were extremely upset to learn of the false charge because it could have caused a major international problem. They asked Ron to prosecute the man in order to clear the air of such a potentially serious incident. But he only wanted to put it behind him. They tried to convince him to no avail.

Stunned, disappointed, hurt at the betrayal, and elated that he had seen the mountain, Ron and the boys headed home where they were met by the news cameras as they arrived in Nashville. Interviewed on "Good Morning

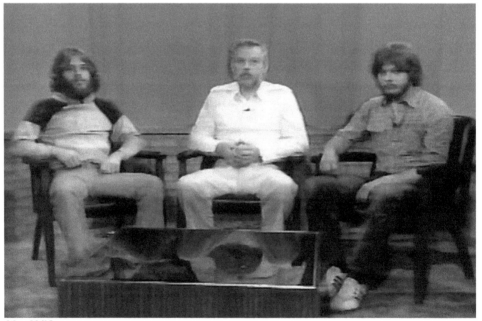

Mary Nell Lee
Danny, Ron and Ronnie in the studio of the Nashville ABC affiliate, WKRN. They were interviewed on "Good Morning America" by Bill Kurtiss.

America", all three were obviously being very careful about what they said.

Ron made the comment that he was not sure that the translator was telling the interrogators what he really said but that is the only negative remark he made. He was not going to speak negatively about their experience. At the same time, he was not willing to ever return there again, at least that is how he felt at the time.

Ron was not one to give up but at the time he settled in his mind that he would not be returning to Saudi Arabia. The experience affected him deeply and caused him to question the wisdom of taking his sons with him to the Middle East. I can personally attest to the fact that he did not want me to change my name on my passport when we got married. He said if anything ever happened, it was best that no one knew we were married.

He set about trying to get back to normal life. He knew the boys, especially Ronnie, had been traumatized and he prayed they would quickly forget the ordeal. But he wouldn't take them overseas after this for a long time.

Telephone call from Saudi

Ron received a very strange telephone call about four or five months later. The voice on the other end identified himself as Samran El Mutairy. He claimed to be a relative of the king of Saudi Arabia. He said he had heard about the mountain from some of the interrogators who had believed Ron's story.

Ever since he had heard about this mountain, he said he couldn't concentrate on anything else. He HAD to see it and Ron had to come back and show it to him. The people Abukahlet had sent out there to investigate the site had obviously gone to the wrong site because they found nothing. He needed Ron.

Ron was polite but adamant that he was not going back to Saudi Arabia but Samran was not to be refused. He boarded a plane and flew to Nashville. He spent several days with Ron and offered to fly him over, cover expenses and provide him a legal visa and protection.

Still, Ron wasn't buying it. He had seen how the Saudis worked. They were strict in their regulations. They had refused to allow Ron to contact the American Embassy or even let his family know where he was the entire time he was imprisoned. He never wanted to be in that position again.

As months went by, Samran continued to call. He lived in Tabuk, just a few hours from the mountain and he wasn't giving up. Finally, Ron invited him to come to Turkey in March of 1985. He was trying to interest Samran in Noah's Ark because Samran kept saying he want to do something for his

Mary Nell Lee
Samran Al Moteri of Tabuk, Saudi Arabia in Nashville when he came to visit Ron in 1984.

god, Allah. Both Mount Sinai and Noah's Ark are mentioned in the Koran and Ron thought he could placate him by showing him Noah's Ark.

Samran met Ron in Ankara. Ron had brought along a new researcher, David Fasold, to Turkey and the three men made their way to Dogubeyazit, Turkey to see the ark site.

David Fasold had brought a metal detecting device and demonstrated it on the ark site as Ron and Samran watched. This device, with David's expertise, detected the pattern of iron lines Ron had gotten with his conventional metal detector provided by White's Electronics. Unfortunately, this only made Samran more adamant that Ron come to Saudi with him.

Ron began to feel more at ease with Samran whom he found to be very personable although he was somewhat grumpy because he was getting over a cold. Samran kept trying to sweeten the pot, to convince Ron to come to Saudi and to also bring David with his metal detector. Samran was fascinated as he watched David Fasold show a pattern of iron lines on the site which would be officially declared to be Noah's Ark by the Turkish government in December of the next year.

Mary Nell Lee
Samran pointing out features on the Noah's ark site with his ever present cigarette in his hand.

They videoed Samran pointing out features on the site and reading about Noah's Ark from his Koran. He was clearly excited. He believed he was on Noah's Ark and this fanned the fire of his fervor for seeing the real Mount Sinai, which was in his own country, close to his home. His excitement was so contagious, Ron could feel himself weakening.

Mary Nell Lee

Samran standing on Noah's Ark in the snow, reading from his Koran.

Finally Ron agreed to go when David agreed to come along. Ron felt safer with someone else along. And Samran wanted David as much as he wanted Ron because David had the magical metal detector.

In order to enter Saudi, a business visa was required. Samran drew up a contract in the hotel in Ankara stating that Ron and David were working for Samran, helping him find commercial minerals using David's specialized equipment. The contract was signed by all on March 31, 1985 and they flew to Jeddah that evening.

Arriving in Jeddah, Samran took Ron's and David's passport and left the line and disappeared to somewhere unknown. Everyone in the airport seemed

AGREEMENT BETWEEN DAVID FASOLD & RONALD WYATT WITH

SAMRAN EL MUTAIRY EST.

Mr. Samran El Mutairy agrees to pay travel expenses and provide Mr Fasold and Mr Wyatt with living quarters and food and transportation while working for his company in The Kingdom of Saudi Arabia; a period of two - three days.

Mr Fasold and Mr Wyatt will provide special mineral detection equipment, and will examin sites to be designated by Mr Samran EL Mutairy and to give him a report of the results of the survey or surveys before the end of two-three days.

Should comercial minerals be located by these surveys, they are to be mined acording to the laws of The Kingdom of Saudi Arabia and whatever profets remain after all claims of The Kingdom of Saudi Arabia are paid, are to be devided between the agreeing parties.

Mr Samran El Mutairy is to recieve seventy five percent of these remaining profits.

Mr. David Fasold and Mr. Ronald Wyatt are to recieve the remaining twenty five percent in the curancy of The Kingdom of Saudi Arabia or of The United States of America: this money to be payed within thirty days of the recient of profits by the office of Mr. Samran EL Mutairy.

SEE WITNESS: SAMRAN EL MUTAIRY

P.S. First step must be jabal alloz (Jabal musa)
    second step must be in the sea   DAVID F. FASOLD

RONALD E. WYATT.

Mary Nell Lee

The contract between Ron, David Fasold and Samran. Little did they know that this legal contract would get them in trouble.

to know Samran and rushed to bow and greet him. This impressed Ron- it seemed that Samran truly was someone of importance.

Then the men were escorted to a waiting limousine where they were taken to the domestic airport. This airport was full of foreign workers from the Phillippines and various African nations along with veiled Saudi women with oversized luggage full of their purchases. Boarding the plane, they made the flight to Tabuk where Samran lived.

Ron described Samran's house as a large compound. It was massive and definitely convinced Ron that Samran was a wealthy and important man. The compound was enclosed in a high wall much like what we saw on the TV of Bin Laden's home several years ago.

Samran had 3 wives and families with each having their own separate household. He had many foreign servants cooking, cleaning, tending the plants and gardens and caring for his fleet of vehicles.

The main portion of the compound was a massive tent. Samran's fleet of vehicles included at least three Mercedes, a Cadillac, and at least three Toyota Land Cruisers. The overall picture was one of great wealth and importance in the region.

The next morning, they left Samran's compound with a full work crew in at least three Land Cruisers and Ron and David in Samran's very expensive Mercedes utility vehicle, and headed to the mountain. Ron tried to direct them to the mountain but he couldn't find the exact location since there were no roads in the desolate region after leaving the main highway at al-Kahn. He had only been a passenger when he visited the mountain a year earlier.

Scott Parvi

This is the landmark formation in the wilderness on the way to the mountain from Al-Kahn that Ron kept looking for. When he finally saw it, they were very close to the mountain.

After a long time of looking for the mountain with no success, they all returned to the highway at al-Kahn where they pulled into the gas station there. When Samran saw a man he knew, he went over to talk to him and suddenly climbed into the man's little Datsun truck. Another driver came over to the Mercedes and slid in to drive.

Suddenly the Datsun took off and everyone quickly fell in behind it. Again driving through deep dust and over large rocks, they set in force a cloud of dust that was probably visible from the moon.

Finally, the Datsun came to a stop. Samran needed some water which was in the Mercedes. As he walked over, he saw a bedouin who was walking over to the cars. They asked him if he knew where Jebel el Lawz was located. He then pointed to the mountain and said "Jebel Musa henna" which meant "Moses' mountain is here." They were at the mountain but were a little north of the area Ron had investigated the year before. As they looked in the direction he pointed, there was a blackened peak that extended across other lower peaks. They then drove further down to the area Ron had seen in 1984 where the altar and other features were.

Jim & Penny Caldwell

Looking down on the altar from the top of the ridge. A chevron-shape, the top "L" is open like a corral. The bottom "L" was rock piled on top of an earthen mound.

The Altar and White Marble Pieces

They walked up to the altar and viewed all the loose pieces of marble that had obviously come from some type of building that had once been there. The bedouin who brought Samran, named Ibrahim Frich, told them the pieces were from a monument that had been removed back in the 1930's. When Ron asked Samran to have him describe what it looked like, he described a round, white, open structure with a curved top. He said he had been told that Suleyman had built it and it had been scavenged to use in building a mosque in Haql.

Ron was able to explore freely and found a piece of flat white marble with Archaic Hebrew writing on it near the altar among the white marble pieces. He knew

Mary Nell Lee
Ibrahim Frich's description of the monument that had once been at the foot of the mountain.

better than to tell anyone about it and ran up the side of the mountain to the right of the altar and buried it under the mass of loose rocks lying everywhere. He slipped and fell in the loose rocks and put a gash in his leg that would leave a scar for the rest of his life.

After seeing the column with Archaic Hebrew and noting as best as he could what the writing looked like, he had determined that the column had the words, "Moses, Mizraim, Pharaoh, Death, Edom, Solomon and Yahweh on it. He believed that it was not Suleyman who had built the white monument but Solomon. Suleyman would not have written in Archaic Hebrew.

Gold Readings in the Area

David stayed near the entrance to the flat area within the mountain and began to use his metal detector. Picking up strong gold readings, he triangulated to 3 spots on the edge of what looked to Ron to be a dried up, artificial lake. Closer examination showed these readings fell within three circles of rocks of 18 foot diameter, each five feet from the other. They would later find a total of 12 of the rock circles. They stopped looking at that point and Ron believed there were more but that is all they located.

They explored the area for a couple of hours but as it got later, they had to leave and the decision was made to spend the night in Haql since it was closer than Tabuk. This made Ron almost sick since his prison was in Haql. He had good reason to be nervous.

Samran had sent his workers back to Tabuk and told them to meet up at the al-Kahn gas station in the morning. Samran then drove Ron and David into Haql. Samran was obviously excited and as soon as he saw someone he knew, he slowed down and hailed them to come speak with him. It was Abukahlet, the chief interrogator of Ron and his sons.

Meeting a Former Interrogator

Samran excitedly began to explain to Abukahlet that Ron Wyatt was now back with a visa and permit and they had been to the mountain and seen all the evidences! But Abukahlet was not pleased. He had sent a team out in 1984 to investigate if there were any remains where Ron said there were and the team came back with nothing. He had forwarded this report to the king.

Abukahlet was by now angry. Then, when Samran ranted on about David's metal detector finding gold readings, it became clear that this was not going to end well.

The 3 men went to the home of a friend of Samran's and though they were not home, their servants gave them a place to sleep. In the middle of the night, two servants came to their room and told Samran they needed to leave. Word was that Ron and David were going to be arrested.

Everyone jumped up and ran to the Mercedes. Heading out onto the dark streets, they became aware of flashing lights behind them. Pulling over, the men from the car behind them ordered them to follow them back to a large compound where they were rushed into an office.

After more than an hour, the men accompanied Samran outside where Ron and David were told to get into a separate car accompanied by two angry looking Arabs. Abukahlet got into the Mercedes with Samran. In order to try to smooth things over, Samran had invited him to come with them to the mountain. Both cars headed to the al-Kahn gas station where Samran's servants were waiting with the Land Cruisers.

Back to the Mountain

Loading into the Land Cruisers, they all headed back to the mountain with Abukahlet and his two assistants. When they arrived, Samran's servants set up to cook and diggers got their shovels and equipment ready to begin whatever work they were told to do.

Workers began to dig down in one of the rock circles where David had gotten a gold reading. These were located along the edge of the man-made lake bed. There were five of them visible although they were eroded and crumbling. Eventually, the diggers would discover they extended 20 feet down into the earth. They were all double walled with smaller rocks placed between the two walls.

Ron concluded they were wells. Being positioned as they were along the top edge of the man-made lake, he believed the water from the lake would seep into the wells and the three layers of rocks would act as a filter providing clean, pure water for the people. His belief was that there were many more along the edge of the lake but all he ever saw were 12.

His belief was that the lake contained the water that flowed from the stream that came from the mountain and the wells were built to provide access to the water. Due to the large number of people, he reasoned that a large number of wells would have been needed.

Randall Lee
2017 photo of one of the rock rings that is situated along the edge of the man-made lake bed.

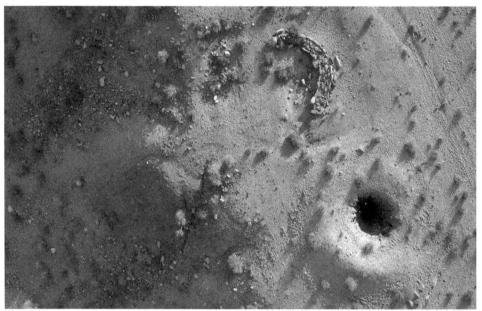

Andrew Jones

Top- 2017 drone photo of the excavated well and one above it. It can be seen they are along the edge of the dry lake bed, visible at left.
Left- 2017 closeup of the 1985 well excavation.
Below- Diagrams showing how the wells were constructed. As water seeped into the well from the lake, the smaller rocks within the double walls would act as a filter.

Randall Lee

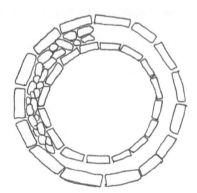

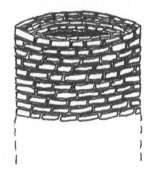

Both drawings- Mary Nell Lee

Tigran Kash

View of the foot of the mountain from the top ridge. A is the area of the camp of the Israelites. B is the location of the golden calf altar. C is the artificial lake dug to contain the water from the spring that originated high atop the mountain. D is the large altar at the foot of the mountain.

Randall Lee

Standing within the man-made dried lake bed. The depth is roughly 25-30 feet although the floor elevation varies.

When it is remembered that the great multitude stayed at Mount Sinai for almost a year, the necessity for a sophisticated water supply becomes obvious. The lake is very large. In the top photo, the stream that originated high up in the mountain is still evidenced by the visible path seen just to the right of D and emptying into the lake C.

Randall Lee
The golden calf altar seen in the foreground surrounded by a 12 foot chain-linked fence. It is approximately 1 km. from the edge of the lake bed.

While the diggers worked at the round rock objects Ron thought were likely wells, Ron and David returned to the site with the etchings of cows amd bulls all over the rocks. There was little doubt in Ron's mind that this was the golden calf altar seen in chapter 3. David's metal detector had picked up very strong gold readings in the direct area of the altar so the men wanted to determine precisely where the reading was strongest. They soon determined the location was within the massive rocks piled upon each other and was not reachable.

The Saudis were trying to keep Ron and David separated most of the time as they surveyed the area and were questioning them just as they had questioned Ron and the boys. Ron realized what was happening and wasn't really surprised when they were suddenly told to get in the car- the work was finished.

Under Arrest Again

Something had been found by the diggers and they were now under arrest. Ron later learned when the diggers had reached about 20 feet down while digging within the round rocks of the well, they had found a gold bracelet. He never learned any more details but in his mind's eye, he could see a Hebrew woman retrieving water from the well. Decked out in the gold jewelry they had gotten from the Egyptians right before they left Egypt, the bracelet came loose from her arm and fell into the well.

It was a "good news, bad news" situation. The gold bracelet proved these were wells as it was the only scenario by which a gold bracelet could be expected to be there when nothing else accompanied it. The bad news was now the Saudis were accusing them of seeking to steal artifacts from their country.

The two men were placed under house arrest at Samran's compound. David was given more freedom than Ron who was confined to his room. Bored and again fearful, he turned on the TV hoping to find something to take his mind off the current predicament. All he found was an Imam reading from the Koran. After about 15 minutes, he turned it off.

A couple of days later, archaeology professor Dr. Saad al-Rashid was flown in from King Saud University. They were able to play David's video for him to view. Even though his video recorder was NTSC and their player was PAL, it still played although in black and white and with no sound.

When the archaeologist saw the bulls and cows on the golden calf altar, he got very excited and said that style of petroglyph was not found anywhere else in Saudi Arabia. He was visibly excited and several times, he shook Ron's hand and congratulated him on his discovery.

The Trial

A day or two later, Ron and David were told they were being taken to the local prince's office in Tabuk. Unknown to them, the person everyone was bowing to was Samran who turned out to be the prince. Also present were members of the interrogation team from Haql including Abukahlet, the archaeologist from Rhiyad, several imams, a translator, the deputy prince and Samran. They all sat in a circle and a trial began.

Ron realized it was imperative to convince them that this was the real Mount Sinai and that was his only reason for searching out the mountain. But he had no idea how to do that so he prayed. As the questioning began, it was the deputy prince who asked Ron why Musa would bring the people to such a miserable location when there were so many better locations in the region? It was a valid point because the region was certainly not conducive to life. This was the reason all the evidence remained relatively in tact all these thousands of years. No one could live in the region year round. Only the Bedouins were there.

There were more questions and one Imam took offense at an answer Ron gave concerning something in the Koran and he decided to not push the point. Praying again, pleading silently for God to help him, Ron began to speak. He repeated the words he had heard the imam speak several days ago during his house arrest.

"Every true Moslem believes every true prophet. If he doesn't believe every true prophet, he isn't a true Moslem." He paused and then asked the group, *"Was not Musa a prophet?"* The eyes of everyone in the room widened and then everyone began nodding and saying *"yes, yes!"*

But the reason for their wide-eyed amazement was not only because of what he had said- but because they all realized the translator had never translated Ron's words. Everyone understood what he was saying! Ron didn't realize at the time that he spoke the words in their language!

They wanted to know how he knew Arabic. He protested that he did not. He swore that he had heard the imam in English. But he was told that was impossible- in Saudi Arabia, it was against the law for the Koran to be read in English. He had understood the words of the Imam, he assumed, in English and had simply repeated the words of the Imam.

This was no small miracle and everyone in the room realized it. They were as shocked as Ron was. The atmosphere was electric and the room erupted in almost chaos. That was the last question asked. It was unanimously agreed by all that this was the true Mount Sinai. The archaeologist again shook Ron's hand and congratulated him on such a major discovery.

But it was not to end as happily as it seemed at the time. The deputy prince then asked Ron to stay and excavate the site. Promises were made that the king would finance the work, that Ron would receive a reward for the discovery, and finally he would be personally introduced to the king.

Ron, though, had to turn down the offer. He had important meetings in Turkey concerning his work there and could not miss them. He had been working on the Noah's Ark site and he was scheduled to meet with all the ministries in Ankara to present his evidence. It was a crucial meeting and it would later result in the December 1986 official announcement that the site was recognized by the Turks as Noah's Ark. The Saudis did not take rejection well.

Kicked Out of the Country, Again

Again, all of their documentation was confiscated. Then they were told to forget they had ever been there. *"And we don't want to read about this in a book or see it in a movie."* Again, he was told to get ready to leave immediately.

Soon after this, the entire area was fenced off by the Saudis and declared protected archaeological sites. It obviously wasn't God's timing for this mountain to be made known. Ron planned on applying to excavate at a later date but that possibility now seemed an impossibility.

The next year, he enlisted his friend, Jim Irwin, the former astronaut, to use his influence and write some letters to the Saudis requesting permission for Ron to return and do the excavation at a later time. He wrote a letter on October 15, 1986 and received a reply from Dr. Abdullah H. Masry, Asst. Dep. Minister for Antiquities and Museum affairs dated November 20, 1986. The letter made it clear that the Saudis no longer were willing to admit this was Mount Sinai. He wrote that they had done a thorough investigation and the site and concluded:

"Our results do not show any relevance to the conclusions referred to the site by Mr. Wyatt, which we believe are archaeologically baseless."

Meanwhile, David Fasold had told two men about his adventure in Saudi Arabia and the evidences at the real Mount Sinai. He admitted to me in a telephone conversation that he had given Bob Cornuke, vice-president of Jim Irwin's organization, High Flight, and Larry Williams detailed directions to the mountain. They had money and connections and were able to get there. They were also able to get out with some photos.

I want to interject here that Ron never believed Jim Irwin was aware of what they were doing even though Mr. Cornuke had been vice president of his organization. It all made sense when Ron recalled that it was Jim Irwin who had called Ron to tell him about David Fasold and ask if he could give David Ron's telephone number. David had contacted Jim to talk to him about using his new metal detecting equipment to search for Noah's Ark in the hardened lava flows at the foot of Mount Ararat. Since Jim was devoted to searching for the ark on the top of Mount Ararat, he thought perhaps David would be a better match for Ron since he was working on a different site. This explained how David Fasold and Bob Cornuke connected.

Mr. Cornuke and Mr. Williams both wrote books claiming they discovered the real Mount Sinai even telling stories similar to Ron's experiences. They later got a published writer to write another book which made Ron look like a bumbling treasure hunter.

But that was just part of life for Ron. The frustration was difficult for him

Mary Nell Lee
Ron, Samran and an unknown man in Nuweiba in February 1988.

because he had seen so much that he believed the world needed to see, not as a great adventure to make people look like heroes but as evidence of the truth of the Bible. Before he died, David called and apologized to Ron for betraying him by giving all the information to Mr. Cornuke and Mr. Williams.

Samran kept in touch with Ron through the ensuing years. He even met Ron in Nuweiba a few times. One day, he told Ron he knew who had Ron's original photos and film and also the video and film from the trip in 1985. The issue was that he wanted something in return.

He continued to stay in touch with Samran hoping that one day he really would get the original photos for him. Samran had all the money in the world so offering him money wouldn't work. However, there were a few things he wanted Ron to get that were not allowed into Saudi. He wanted Ron to arrange to get those things to him in return for all the photos and videos. Some of the things he wanted, I will not mention as they were not things we could get for him. But one thing he wanted was a set of long-range walkie-talkies. They were expensive back then, but we could get them.

Back in the 1980's and early 1990's, long-range two-way radios were outlawed in Saudi. They were actually difficult to get in the U.S. as well, but could be bought for a high price. The problem would be getting them into Saudi Arabia. A plan was devised to get them to Samran but he was not making it easy to get it accomplished. Ron began to wonder if he really could get the confiscated items to Ron or not.

Divine Intervention in Nuweiba

There is always talk about miracles among Christians. Some people get "turned off" by the very word. But miracles DO happen. After seeing all the evidence at Mount Sinai, Ron's heart was burdened greatly. He believed if people could only see everything there, it would strengthen their faith. Even Biblical scholars proclaimed the story of the Exodus was not true and Mount Sinai was therefore not identifiable. He couldn't understand why God had allowed him to go through so much and not have anything to show people. But he always trusted and knew that God had His Own timetable.

Finally the miracle happened he had waited for. In January of 1992, Ron and I took two Korean doctors to Egypt and Israel as they wanted to see the sites of Ron's discoveries. In Nuweiba one evening Ron tried to called Samran in Tabuk, Saudi Arabia. Ron had been talking to Samran from the U.S. and was supposed to get in touch with him when we arrived in Nuweiba. But every time Ron tried to call Samran, he wasn't home and one of his wives would answer the phone and none of them spoke English.

The manager of the hotel in Nuweiba Ahmed Samy, overheard the calls as they had to be made in the office. He told Ron he would be happy to help him with the calls since he spoke both English and Arabic.

This led to Ron telling him why he was calling Samran and about Mount Sinai. Samy, as we called him, then told Ron he could go over and get photos for him because he had never used his Haj visa. He explained that all Moslems are allowed to go to Saudi Arabia to Mecca for Haj once in their lives.

The first miracle of that trip was the fact that I had made a copy of a map of the mountain and brought it with us. I had never done that before and didn't even think about why I was doing it at the time.

I gave Ron the map and he asked me to draw some landmarks on a piece of paper for Samy so he could recognize when he was at the right location. I drew the distinctive boulders on top of the mountain that had a single tree between them. This was a very unique distinction that set the correct

Nathan Bange

Above and below- The most unique feature and identifier for the correct site was a lone tree setting between two large boulders upon a minor peak at the mountain.

Scott Parvi

mountain apart in this massive mountain range. The area contains mountain after mountain and there had to be something to distinguish it.

Then I drew some stone circles where Ron had seen ancient settlements. Finally I drew a crude Egyptian style bull like he had seen on the golden calf altar. I had never seen these before but Ron had sketched them years earlier and I was a better artist, he said. He then gave the map to Samy and agreed to pay him handsomely if he was successful. We also gave him $1,500 and left him a camera.

Soon after arriving back home from that trip a couple of weeks later, we received a call from Samy asking us to wire more money. It was going to cost $2,000 more. Now, I will be honest- I believed we had already wasted $1,500 and a perfectly good camera so I protested. But Ron told me to wire the money.

I went to the bank and made the wire at 1:30 that day. At 5:20, the bank called and said the wire did not go through and that I needed to check and see if there was an additional account number to go with the one I had used. I had prayed that God would stop the wire if this was not going to work and I was satisfied that this was the answer. But Ron had his own way of doing things. He tried something 3 times before he gave up. So I called Samy and he gave me another number he had failed to give me before.

I called the bank the next morning to give them the additional account number and they informed me that I had to come in person. However, they said the wire system was down and I needed to come in later in the afternoon before wires shut down at 2:00.

As I waited to leave in time to get there by 1:30, the phone rang. Ron happened to be home and he answered it. I could tell by the look on his face that it was a strange call. When he hung up, he told me it a was lady who said her brother lived in Saudi Arabia. Her brother had asked her to find "Ron Wyatt" who lived in Nashville and was working in the Middle East. She then told Ron she had no idea what it was about but her brother needed Ron to call him right away.

Ron, of course, called him immediately and the man told him a very strange tale. This man, Jim Caldwell, and his family were Americans who lived in Saudi Arabia. He worked there and had been on a required vacation touring Egypt.

They had started their trip at the hotel we were at in Nuweiba, although they arrived a couple of weeks before we did. They then drove to the traditional Mount Sinai in the Sinai Peninsula. Disillusioned at what they saw, they developed a strong desire to see the real Mount Sinai, wherever it was. They bought several books on the subject discussing different theories and began to study them.

As their vacation came to an end, they returned to the hotel in Nuweiba about 30 minutes after we had left. Then the story got even more amazing. After he had finished talking, Ron immediately made airline reservations to meet them in Bahrain.

On Feb. 23, 1992 Ron met them in his hotel room and videoed Jim, his wife Penny and their two young children. Jim told the following story:

"About 5:30, we arrive in Nuweiba to almost what I would consider a hero's welcome!... We pulled up, we had not been there for 22 days, we pull up, Ahmed Samy comes running out , he's welcoming us back, I mean, and hugging on us, Mohammed as well, same thing…

Mohammed gives us his best suite, complimentary, for two days… I mean, I was taken away. So we're sitting down having some Turkish coffee and Ahmed Samy says 'Jim, I got, I've got something I gotta tell you. I need to talk to you but it's gotta be alone.'

Well, I mean it set me back because I barely knew this guy. I thought, here it comes, once alone, my check bounced, something happened, right? And they're gonna own my truck and we'll have to go back across on the ferry on our own. I didn't know- I had no idea.

So he comes out to the truck with me and he says, he says that, I've got this incredible news. He says, 'There's this ark, this man that discovered the ark. And he said, and he thinks there's something over there, in Arabia, and I have a map', and anyway his story got real clustered and I couldn't follow what he was saying.

I thought he was saying Ark of the Covenant. Then I said, no he must be talking about Noah's Ark. And he said your name. Your name didn't sink in, ok, to be honest with you. My memory for names is real bad. It had been a year and a half since I had seen the video, now, so you gotta understand. [Someone had sent Jim a video of an interview of Ron talking about the discovery of Noah's Ark. He explained that VHS tapes were checked by the Saudis and all religious programs were confiscated. But 8mm tapes, which were fairly new at that time, always arrived. So he asked his family and friends to always send 8mm tapes. Then when he received them, he would copy the tape to VHS format and reuse the tape in his recorder.]

So I said, golly, I don't know. So he went on and he said he had this map of where it was and everything. So things started being pieced together and he wanted to show me this map later on and I said ok.

So I went back in and Penny, by this time, I started to realize what he was talking about, and Penny, when she saw my face, when I came back in, she knew, she said it was like I had seen a ghost. I mean, I was just white.

Penny- He was aghast.

Jim- I was, I was totally overwhelmed. It was starting to sink in. He had either found the real Mount Sinai or the Ark of the Covenant was there, or something. But all these things I had been thinking about and dreaming about were kinda coming together. So he uh, a little later on, he shows us this map that you had drawn. And I swear I almost passed out. I saw that map , I swear it was just like God had drawn it with His Hand and said, "look here it is. If you want to find it, here it is.". ...

So he started on more about you, and some of the things that had gone on. He wasn't saying your name, he was real reserved about giving me information.

Penny- I asked him at dinner, "What was his name"?...

Jim- Finally she gets the name out of him and we start thinking about it, and I started making a connection to you. It started coming together.

The Noah's Ark, there's some info,…. Here's the way he put it, there's some information at this mountain, at Mount Sinai, that connected to Noah's Ark. Well, the only thing that connected was you. You were the guy that had found Noah's Ark and now this real Mount Sinai. There were no inscriptions in the mountain that said "Noah's Ark",…. This is the way it was coming from Ahmed Samy.

But, so I finally said, well you know, I've shot more video, home video, on this trip than I ever had. I had 10 tapes with me. And I had shot 9 two-hour tapes. I had one left. And I just rewrite over these things over and over again.

Penny- At random…

*Jim- I went to my bag, and I was thinking, I used to have that, you know, on 8mm. I wonder, then I said, naw, I probably wrote over it. But I reached in my bag and I got my last video tape out. I put it in, I put the thing on VCR and I started it rolling, **and there is your face in this interview!***

*And I held it up to Ahmed's face, and he went **"That's him"**! I almost passed out, … Ahh! It was just amazing! Again, it was a sleepless night!*

He made arrangements with me to go over and make the video and said that this is what you wanted, of the area, and he showed me the circles, the bulls and the tree and the rocks, all of the area, and he said, this is what the man wants video of. And I was to bring it to his brother. Then he [Ahmed Samy] would fly in on a Haj visa and pick it up. And then, finished. And we agreed to it. We did, we said all we wanted, basically we had, what we wanted, we had a map, we want to go there and walk

Penny- We knew that God was leading us to do this and after seeing the map, the physical evidence, we knew we were not daydreaming.

The videotape of their meeting is long and cannot be included in its entirety here but their story was very exciting to say the least.

Jim went on to explain how he and his family went to the mountain and with all the proper paperwork, they were able to travel freely in the area. They videoed and photographed everything they saw. Then when they returned to their home in Saudi, they called Jim's sister and had her find Ron. As a result, Ron met them in Bahrain and they gave Ron all their photos and videos, including the negatives.

In this same video, Ron told them, *"If you come in to Rephidim, which is almost directly west, uh, you were in the area to the north and to the south, and over to the east, … but right over that area, the back of the mountain, down below is Rephidim. And I don't know if they have people posted there to watch for people or not."*

Scott Parvi

The "rock at Horeb" where a massive amount of water come from between the crack. The rock is about 60 feet tall, sitting on an approximately 100 feet-plus hill. You can see Scott at the bottom center.

The Caldwells returned, went to that location, and made another very exciting discovery- the rock of Horeb which was at Rephidim where Moses struck the rock and water came out. This very exciting evidence proves that a massive amount of water came out, not just a little stream. It was mind boggling!

They continued to go to the region and document it for Ron. They came to our home in Nashville and brought more. Once they sent video and photos with friends who were visiting in Tennessee. They had to remain anonymous during the time they lived in Saudi and we were not allowed to reveal their identities. This continued for a while but finally came to an end when they later decided to team up with other people who could promote it to a larger audience. They had provided Ron with more than he had ever dreamed of having and he was eternally grateful to them. No one could have done a better job than they did.

As for Samy and his scheme, we continued to see him through the years. Although he didn't get the photos and videos for us, we paid him when he needed to get another vehicle. After all, it never would have happened without his kind offer to help Ron with his conversations with Samran's wives.

But there was still a problem. It was obvious that the Saudis did not want this known. After they had time to think about it, they decided it was not in their best interest. And Ron understood why. He was familiar with the belief that some people had that the Jewish people had a right to any land their feet had trod upon:

Deu. 11:24 Every place whereon the soles of your feet shall tread shall be yours; from the wilderness and Lebanon, from the river, the river Euphrates, even unto the uttermost sea shall your coast be.

However, when read in context, it can be seen that this is a conditional promise whose conditions they failed to fulfill:

Deu 11:22 For if ye shall diligently keep all these commandments which I command you, to do them, to love the LORD your God, to walk in all his ways, and to cleave unto him; 23 Then will the LORD drive out all these nations from before you, and ye shall possess greater nations and mightier than yourselves. 24 Every place whereon the soles of your feet shall tread shall be yours: from the wilderness and Lebanon, from the river, the river Euphrates, even unto the uttermost sea shall your coast be. 25 There shall no man be able to stand before you: for the LORD your God shall lay the fear of you and the dread of you upon all the land that ye shall tread upon, as he hath said unto you.

Ron wrote a long letter to the Saudis and tried to address the issue but never heard back from them. In this excerpt from that letter, he wrote:

"The fear of seizure and occupation of this historic site by the Israelis is not totally unreasonable. For example, Jewish and Christian historians have overlooked or deliberately ignored the historically documentable fact that the descendants of Jacob (Israel) were a mere fraction (one-tenth to one-twelfth) of the ethnic groups, if not numerical components, of the followers of the prophet Moses. The descendants of Ishamel, the six sons of Katura (the third wife of Abraham), Dedan, Sheba, Midian, etc., also some of the descendants of Esau, have a much greater claim to the sites of the events of the Exodus than do the Israelis.

The non-Israeli participants in the Exodus were referred to in the Hebrew/Josephus history of the Exodus as the 'mixed multitude' who are noticeably absent from the ranks of the migrating Habiru after the encamping (approximately one year's duration) at Horeb. These long unrecognized and unheralded participants in the Exodus were the ancestors of the peoples of the modern R. K. S. A. and the Arabian Gulf States."

The evidence at Mount Sinai is overwhelming in both size and details. It proves that a major event took place there. It fits the Biblical description. It is across the Gulf of Aqaba from where Ron found the chariot parts.

In the 1990's, the Saudis excavated the altar complex and removed all the earth that was within the leg labeled B in the below diagram. When Ron saw the altar in 1984 and 1985, he said it was filled with earth and overlaid with rocks around it. This agrees with the command God gave to Moses in Exodus of how to build an altar to Him:

Exo. 20:24 **An altar of earth** *thou shalt make unto me, and shalt sacrifice thereon thy burnt offerings, and thy peace offerings, thy sheep, and thine oxen: in all places where I record my name I will come unto thee, and I will bless thee. 25 And* **if thou wilt make me an altar of stone, thou shalt not build it of hewn stone**: *for if thou lift up thy tool upon it, thou hast polluted it.*

It was Ron's belief, based on seeing the altar complex before it was excavated, the section B seen in the diagram below was filled with earth and was the altar portion of the complex since God had commanded an altar of earth.

In the Saudi's report, they found evidence of organic material and ash in the areas to the right which would be expected if this were an altar. However, they have chosen to state that it was a housing complex for marble workers.

Scott Parvi

In the 1990's, the Saudis excavated the altar complex. They assumed the right leg (B in the diagram below) matched the left (A in the below diagram) and they removed the earth and arranged the rocks to make it look the same.

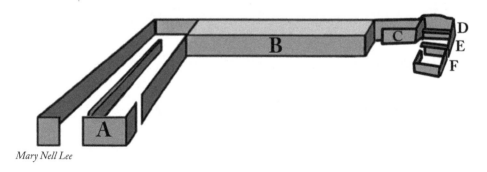

Mary Nell Lee

Ron believed the A portion of the complex was where the people entered with their sacrificial animals. When they reached the top end where it joined with the B segment, they handed their sacrificial animal to a priest and then exited down the other side of the divided corridor.

Another feature of the mountain that is vital to its identification as Mount Sinai is an area fitting for the 70 elders to have waited while Moses met with God and received the Tables of Stone:

Exo. 24:9 Then went up Moses, and Aaron, Nadab, and Abihu, and seventy of the elders of Israel: 10 And they saw the God of Israel: and there was under his feet as it were a paved work of a sapphire stone, and as it were the body of heaven in his clearness. 11 And upon the nobles of the children of Israel he laid not his hand: also they saw God, and did eat and drink. 12 And the LORD said unto Moses, Come up to me into the mount, and be there: and I will give thee tables of stone, and a law, and commandments which I have written; that thou mayest teach them. 13 And Moses rose up, and his minister Joshua: and Moses went up into the mount of God. 14 And he said unto the elders, Tarry ye here for us, until we come again unto you: and, behold, Aaron and Hur are with you: if any man have any matters to do, let him come unto them. 15 And Moses went up into the mount, and a cloud covered the mount.

Nathan Bange
The plateau above the altar area. Large enough for the 70 elders. The mountain top is seen.

In 1997, Viveka Pontén of Sweden moved to Tabuk so that she could continue to research the area for Ron. Several of her photographs are in this book including two photographs in the waters just off the beach on page 18.

God had His Own time for these things to be revealed. Today, Saudi Arabia has opened their doors to tourism. My husband, Randall, has been there several times. He was told a story about a man who lived near the mountain by his son. This man's father had a tent close to the base of the mountain and ran a small business. One night, he was awoken by noise and went outside to see what was going on. What he saw nearly frightened him to death.

He saw 3 men, all about 15 feet tall, dressed in dark Arabian winter garb. They floated from there to the foot of the mountain and then rose up into the sky and disappeared. The poor man fell to the ground in great fear and rolled up into a ball. He was asking people what this meant but I don't know that anyone would have the answer to that.

One of his foreign hired hands also came out and saw the three men and he fled the area. To the best of my knowledge, has never returned.

Getting the evidence to show others was truly a battle for which Ron fought and paid a great price. But God proved that He was in charge. More and more scholars are accepting that this is the true Mountain of God.

Years after it happened, Ron still spoke of seeing that column on the beach in Saudi and how overwhelming it was to see it setting there. He firmly believed it saved his life as his captors simply did not believe his story. But when they saw that column, their attitude changed.

He remained in awe of how the room full of Saudis looked at him with wide-eyes as he spoke the words of the imam from the TV. He said he was not aware that he was speaking in Arabic. He was as completely shocked as they were. But he remembered the words of Jesus:

Mar. 13:9 But take heed to yourselves: for they shall deliver you up to councils; and in the synagogues ye shall be beaten: and ye shall be brought before rulers and kings for my sake, for a testimony against them.... 11 But when they shall lead you, and deliver you up, take no thought beforehand what ye shall speak, neither do ye premeditate: but whatsoever shall be given you in that hour, that speak ye: for it is not ye that speak, but the Holy Ghost.

The incident in Nuweiba with Samy and the Caldwell family was no coincidence. Only God could have arranged that. Only then was it His time for the mountain to be seen.

Chapter 19

BATTLE FOR JERICHO

One of the first places Ron took me to see was Jericho. He believed there was a wealth of evidence there pointing directly to the Biblical account of Joshua and Israel taking Jericho and the miraculous manner in which the walls fell. But there has been a real battle for the truth about this city as well.

Evidence of Israel Entering Canaan

There is no direct evidence of the entry of the Israelites into Canaan according to scholars and archaeologists. Many writers have set forth their belief that the Amarna Letters tell of events as the Israelites entered Canaan, but Ron did not agree. The accumulation of letters ended when the Amarna family died out before Israel entered Canaan.

If the number of years of the reigns of Ay, Akhenaton and Horemheb are accurately reflected in the dated inscriptions available, allowing Ay 4 years; Akhenaton 17 years; and Horemheb 14 years, this is a total of 35 years. This would bring the date to just 5 years before the entry into Canaan. But it is most likely that there were some half years and silent years involved which could bring the date to or past the time of the conquest of the Promise Land.

In addition, there is the possibility that there was time unaccounted for prior to the accession of Ay, time when the question of what to do was being debated. But the letters that accumulated at Amarna came to end when the family died out. As a result, most scholars and archaeologists state emphatically that there is no evidence of the Biblical account of the children of Israel entering Canaan and conquering the land. But I protest there IS actually strong evidence for at least one major event.

The battle of scholars and archaeologists against the truth of the Bible cannot be seen any clearer than when reviewing the evidence at Jericho. The story is told in Joshua chapter 6. To briefly recap, the city was destroyed when priests of the Most High carried the Ark of the Covenant on their shoulders and marched around the city of Jericho with armed men of Joshua's army.

Jericho was a stronghold city that guarded the entry into Canaan from the east. Like other Canaanite cities, it was built with a strong Canaanite double wall. Being located just north of the Dead Sea, it was also the lowest city on earth at 670 feet below sea level.

The remains of the ancient city are destroyed. The walls have fallen outward. The city is blackened by the conflagration that completed its destruction. The evidences from the excavations provide a wealth of facts which are entirely consistent with the Biblical account.

Excavations of Jericho

The destruction of Jericho marked the first event upon the great multitudes' entry into Canaan. After being excavated by three separate teams, a great battle ensued for the truth revealed by those excavations. The first excavation took place in 1907 by Austrian and German archaeologists Ernst Sellin and Carl Watzinger. Their original conclusion was that the city was not even occupied at the time the Israelites entered Canaan.

John Garstang then led his excavation from 1930 to 1936 and Sir Charles Marston wrote about that excavation and documented the results. Amazingly, one of the first evidences, the pottery sherds he discussed, failed to meet the criteria of the Exodus date because even at that early time, most scholars were of the opinion that the date for the entry into Canaan was about 1220 BC:

"This evidence for the correctness of the Book of Joshua was, however, overshadowed by the fact that the potsherds supplied a date of about 1400 B.C." ("New Bible Evidence From the 1925-1933 Excavations" by Sir Charles Marston, p. 129)

Public Domain

The revement or rampart around the raised mound of the city of Jericho. The first wall sat on top of this revement. In front of this, outside the city, was an approximately nine foot dry moat around the entire city.

Public Domain

A close up of the revement surrounding ancient Jericho.

From this evidence, the correct date was originally determined and they discounted it! That was amazing. Archaeologists have continued to discount the original work done at Jericho which showed clearly that it was destroyed in precisely the manner described in the Bible by Joshua:

"So great was the importance of verifying the date of the destruction, that in 1930, Professor Garstang and his wife cleaned and examined no fewer than

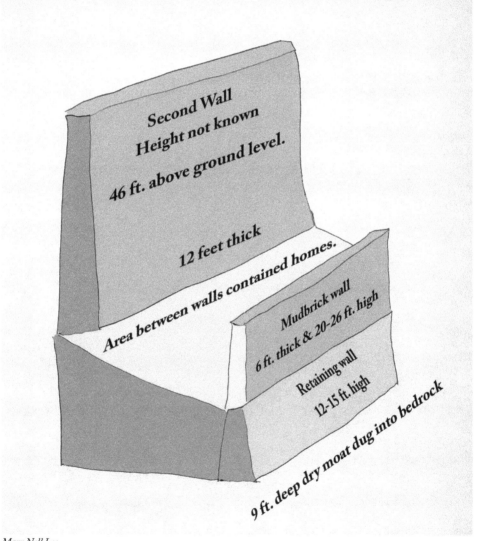

Mary Nell Lee

A diagram of the basic construction of the wall surrounding ancient Jericho. This is a typical Canaanite design and would provide solid protection against attackers. The height of the second wall is not known due to the city's complete destruction and collapse of that wall.

sixty thousand fragments from the strata of the burned city. At the expedition in the following year (1931) another forty thousand fragments were treated in a similar manner. They all attested to the same date, that of the middle of the late Bronze Age (1400 BC) before the infiltration of the Mykenean ware." (Marston, p. 135.)

Garstang wrote in his book about his excavation, "The Story of Jericho":

"*The main defenses of Jericho in the Late Bronze Age [LB] followed the upper brink of the city mound, and comprised two parallel walls, the outer six feet and the inner twelve feet thick. Investigations along the west side show continuous signs of destruction and conflagration. The outer wall suffered most, its remains falling down the slope. The inner wall is preserved only where it abuts the citadel, or tower, to a height of eighteen feet; elsewhere it is found largely to have fallen, together with the remains of buildings upon it, into the space between the walls which was filled with ruins and debris. Traces of intense fire are plain to see, including reddened masses of brick, cracked stones,*

The exposed city of ancient Jericho after the walls had fallen. The outside wall sat atop the revetment seen along the outside edge of the remains.

charred timber and ashes. Houses alongside the wall were found burnt to the ground, their roofs fallen upon the domestic pottery within."

The Biblical account tells that not only did the walls fall, but the Israelites then burned it completely, the exact evidence he documented.

The remains of food supplies were found:

"In another room abutting the same western wall, but more to the south, the traces of fire upon its walls were as fresh as though it had occurred a

Large storage jugs full of grain in the remains of ancient Jericho.

month before; each scrape of the trowel exposed a black layer of charcoal, where the roof had burned, or caused the piled up ashes to run down in a stream. On a brick ledge in a corner of this room we found the family provision of dates, barley, oats, olives, an onion and pepper-corns, all charred but unmistakable; while a little store of bread, together with a quantity of unbaked dough which had been laid aside to serve as leaven for the morrow's baking, told plainly the same tale of a people cut off in full activity."

The destruction of Jericho was quick and sudden, not expected. Everything was left behind exactly as it had been just before the walls fell. It was a perfect picture of the Biblical description.

The Biblical account tells that the spies who had gone into the city, were harbored and protected by Rahab. This is a very important part of the Biblical account because Rahab is later found in the genealogy of Jesus.

The two spies promised Rahab her family would be delivered from the terrible destruction that lay ahead. In time, the Israelites followed the directions of God for the taking of the city:

Jos 6:20 So the people shouted when the priests blew with the trumpets: and it came to pass, when the people heard the sound of the trumpet, and the people shouted with a great shout, that the wall fell down flat, so that the people went up into the city, every man straight before him, and they took the city. 21 And they utterly destroyed all that was in the city, both man and woman, young and old, and ox, and sheep, and ass, with the edge of the sword. **22 But Joshua had said unto the two men that had spied out the country, Go into the harlot's house, and bring out thence the woman, and all that she hath, as ye sware unto her. 23 And the young men that were spies went in, and brought out Rahab, and her father, and her mother, and her brethren, and all that she had; and they brought out all her kindred, and left them without the camp of Israel.** *24 And they burnt the city with fire, and all that was therein: only the silver, and the gold, and the vessels of brass and of iron, they put into the treasury of the house of the LORD. 25 And Joshua saved Rahab the harlot alive, and her father's household, and all that she had; and she dwelleth in Israel even unto this day; because she hid the messengers, which Joshua sent to spy out Jericho.*

The German team who exacavated in 1907 found an interesting feature on the north wall, an eight foot tall section was still standing. Since Rahab's house was built against the outer wall, this was highly likely to have been where her house was located. This is an amazing confirmation of the precise details in the Biblical account.

Garstang then asked British archaeologist, Kathleen Kenyon, to review his findings and conclusions. This led to her undertaking of another excavation from 1952 to 1958. She agreed that her findings confirmed Garstang's earlier work. She found the evidence of a double wall, that the walls had fallen outward, that the city had been thoroughly burned and that there were massive amounts of stored grain still present. However, she concluded that the destruction of Jericho took place in about 1570 BC by the fleeing Hyksos or that it was destroyed by the Egyptians.

Then another archaeologist became interested in Jericho- Bryant Wood. He carefully studied the excavation reports of Garstang and Kenyon. He finally concluded that the evidence depicted the event of the destruction of Jericho exactly as depicted in the Biblical account. In his article in BAR, he summarized the evidence and wrote:

"...The correlation between the archaeological evidence and the Biblical narrative is substantial:
 • *The city was strongly fortified (Joshua 2:5,7,15, 6:5,20).*
 • *The attack occurred just after spring harvest time (Joshua 2:6, 3:15, 5:10).*
 • *The inhabitants had no opportunity to flee with their foodstuffs (Joshua 6:1).*

Randall Lee
The only section of the outside wall that remained standing. It is on the north side of the city and was most likely the location of the home of Rahab.

- *The siege was short (Joshua 6:15).*
- *The walls were leveled, possibly by an earthquake (Joshua 6:20).*
- *The city was not plundered (Joshua 6:17-18).*
- *The city was burned (Joshua 6:20)."*

(Biblical Archaeology Review, Vol. XVI, No. 2, March/April 1990, pp. 44-58 by Bryant Wood)

He went on to explain why the presence of grain in the remains of the collapsed and burned remains is such an important evidence:

"The most abundant item found in the destruction, apart from pottery, was grain. As noted above, both Garstang and Kenyon found large quantities of

Mary Nell Lee
Ron and I visiting the remains of the destroyed city of Jericho.

grain stored in the ground-floor rooms of the houses. In her limited excavation area, Kenyon recovered six bushels of grain in one season! This is unique in the annals of Palestinian archaeology. Perhaps a jar or two might be found, but to find such an extensive amount of grain is exceptional. What conclusions can we draw from this unusual circumstance?

Grain was a very valuable commodity in antiquity. The amount stored after harvest provided food until the next harvest. Grain was so valuable, in fact, that it was used as a medium of exchange. The presence of these grain stores in the destroyed city is entirely consistent with the Biblical account. The city did not fall as a result of a starvation siege, as was so common in ancient times. Instead, the Bible tells us, Jericho was destroyed after but seven days (Joshua 6:15,20). Successful attackers normally plundered valuable grain once they captured a city. This of course would be inconsistent with the grain found here. But in the case of Jericho, the Israelites were told that "the city and all that is within it shall be devoted to the Lord for destruction," and they were commanded, "Keep yourselves from the things devoted to destruction" (Joshua 6:17-18). So the Israelites were forbidden to take any plunder from Jericho. This could explain why so much grain was left to burn when City IV met its end." (Wood)

Another VERY Strong Evidence

Equally exciting was the discovery of the cemetery of this city:

"In due course a number of tombs were opened that proved to belong to the century 1500- 1400 BC. and included royal tombs of the period. There were found a succession of eighty scarabs bearing the cartouches of the eighteenth dynasty Pharaohs. In one was unearthed scarabs bearing the joint names of Princess Hatshepsut and Thotmes III (1501- 1487 BC.) and in another two royal seals of Amenhetep III....As the series of dated scarabs all come to an end with the two royal seals of Amenhetep III, there is evidence, quite independent of the pottery, that the city also ceased to exist during that period." (Marston, pp. 136 and 137.)

The scarabs are the strongest possible evidence that the city came to an end after Amenhotep III, the pharaoh of the Exodus. In the intervening years after the Exodus and before the destruction of Jericho, there was dwindling evidence of Egypt in Canaan. There were no powerful pharaohs to rule over the vassals in the region who were falling prey to other attackers. There were no artisans in Egypt to make scarabs of the pharaohs to be spread near and far. All Egypt could do until the destruction of Jericho was struggle to survive.

If Egypt had maintained her vassals in Canaan and kept their fortresses fully protected with Egyptian troops, it would have greatly hindered the children of Israel as they came into the promised land to possess it. The timing of events can only be described as arranged by the Hand of God.

The evidences gleaned from the excavation of Jericho are completely compelling. The city was destroyed in the exact manner described in the Bible. The discovery of the only section of wall being preserved is another very strong confirmation of the story of Rahab. This is conclusive evidence that the city was destroyed at the end of the 18th Dynasty, the same dynasty Ron first determined to be connected with the Exodus because of the discovery of the chariot remains he saw in 1978.

Chapter 20

CONCLUSION

It is impossible to completely understand an ancient people and culture with only an incomplete record of their existence left for us to examine. But as I have stated, I believe in the Bible and the truth it contains. I believe that the God of Abraham and Moses preserved exactly what was needed to prove His point.

The key to understanding ancient history is having a sound basis on which to build. The events of the 18th Dynasty portrayed the life of Moses through the Exodus when applied to a Biblical basis. The understanding that during this dynasty the pharaohs had different names for their position as co-regent and emperor pharaoh brought it all into focus. Although I have only given other dynasties a cursory look, I believe this policy of co-regents and senior pharaohs having different names was practiced in a number of other dynastic families.

There is a verse in the Bible which indicates that Egypt had more than one king at a time:

*Jer 46:25 The LORD of hosts, the God of Israel, saith; Behold, I will punish the multitude of No, and Pharaoh, and Egypt, with their gods, and their **kings;** even Pharaoh, and all them that trust in him:*

There is so much we still don't understand about these ancient people.

Discovery of the Hittites

Consider the subject of the Hittites. The Bible spoke of a powerful nation called the Hittites. Yet until the 1800's, skeptics used this as proof the Bible wasn't trustworthy because no evidence had ever been found of such a people.

Then in the 1800's, different people began to find evidences in an ancient city in Turkey called Bogazkoy. Stones with ancient writing were removed against the protests of the local residents who held superstitions that the stones held magical properties to cure eye diseases. But with military help, some of the stones were removed to the governor's palace.

That night the "Whirling Dervishes" danced through the streets as a shower of falling stars further enraged the crowd who saw it as an omen that Allah was displeased with the removal of the stones. A crowd stormed the palace and was still there in the morning. The governor calmed the crowd and sent the stones to the Istanbul Museum. But the stones and their writings were still a mystery.

Meanwhile in 1876, excavations at ancient Carchemish revealed monuments of the same style and writing which contained the same mysterious hieroglyphs. Scholar Archibald Henry Sayce first concluded that these monuments were those of the ancient Biblical Hittites.

More evidence came and the positive identification was made. Part of that evidence was the Amarna Letters which helped put many pieces of the puzzle into their correct perspective.

This very exciting story of the discovery of the great Hittite nation whose absence from the archaeological records was used for a long time to discredit the Bible can be read in the article entitled "The Hittites- A Civilization Lost and Found" by David Down, in "Archaeological Diggings", Vol. 23, No. 3, May 2016.

When something is needed for His people, God provides just enough to "be enough" for honest hearted people who will benefit; people who want the truth. Sadly, I have concluded that most people don't really want the truth but there are still those who have not "bowed the knee to Baal." Then there are those who have heard so many lies and fables that they just need some evidence which they will thankfully grasp.

The discovery of the chariot parts has been discounted by many people since Ron never brought anything to the surface except the hub he gave to Dr. Hassan and which is now lost. But what Ron saw in the waters off Nuweiba beach convinced him of two things- he absolutely believed that the Exodus had to occur in the 18th Dynasty and it convinced him that the Red Sea crossing happened at the Gulf of Aqaba which meant that Mount Sinai was in present day Saudi Arabia. Today, Mount Sinai is visited by tourists every day since the Saudi government opened the country to tourism. It is guarded closely but it is still possible to see it. This, to me, is a miracle, just one of so many.

The evidence of the 18th Dynasty is overwhelming. The preservation of Tutankhamun's tomb which captured the attention of the entire world is like nothing that has been found before or after. Prior to its discovery, Tutankhamun was not even well-known to archaeologists. The preservation of Hatshepsut's mortuary temple, Djeser-Djeseru, is another example of what I believe to be Divine preservation. The discovery of Senenmut's (Moses') parents' tomb is one of the most exciting subjects one could imagine. The large amount of statues and inscriptions of and about Senenmut/Thutmose II has given us more than a glimpse into the life of Moses as a young man in the courts of ancient Egypt. And the list goes on.

The theory Ron described to me 32 years ago fits the Biblical account. It forms a pattern and all pieces of the puzzle have been included and fit. It presents a picture of Egypt before, during, and after the Exodus. It reveals exciting details and provides glimpses of some of the people we have long read about in the Scriptures.

If there was ever a time when the world needed evidence of His Truth, it is now. All the evidences preserved for such a time as this, when the Bible is completely discounted as having any relevance to history, can only be attributed to the Hand of God.

This does not eliminate the need for faith. As we see every day, people can explain away anything and everything if they don't want to know the truth. Sometimes, a little confirmation can go a long way for someone who has been struggling with their faith. If God provides something for us, we can be assured we need it.

The times we live in are uncertain. The world is against the Truth. We need to have complete confidence in his Word. God made a statement that surely applies to today more than ever:

Jer. 16:19 O LORD, my strength, and my fortress, and my refuge in the day of affliction, the Gentiles shall come unto thee from the ends of the earth, and shall say, Surely our fathers have inherited lies, vanity, and things wherein there is no profit. 20 Shall a man make gods unto himself, and they are no gods? 21 **Therefore, behold, I will this once cause them to know, I will cause them to know mine hand and my might; and they shall know that my name is The LORD.**

INDEX

Acknowledgements

I am extremely grateful to Scott Parvi for working with me the entire time I was writing this book. He was my proofreader and brought my attention to things I needed to address with more information. I was honored that he agreed to write the introduction.

I also owe a debt of gratitude to Molly Hickman and Tammy Gose for reading the book and providing much needed guidance on items that needed to be expounded upon and/or better organized. It's difficult for a writer to write on a subject they have been studying for over 30 years and present it in a manner that someone with no background in the subject can understand.

Finally I thank my husband, Randall Lee, who made it possible for me to write without interruption. He was my cheerleader, encouraging me when I felt I just couldn't get it done. He cooked and cleaned. He went to Egypt and Saudi Arabia and got specific photographs I needed.

Thank you all for your help and support.

Printed in the USA
CPSIA information can be obtained
at www.ICGtesting.com
LVHW061754100124
768426LV00028B/1685